George Cary Eggleston

How to Educate Yourself

With or Without Masters

George Cary Eggleston

How to Educate Yourself
With or Without Masters

ISBN/EAN: 9783744734592

Printed in Europe, USA, Canada, Australia, Japan

Cover: Foto ©Paul-Georg Meister /pixelio.de

More available books at **www.hansebooks.com**

How to Educate Yourself:

WITH OR WITHOUT MASTERS.

BY

GEO. CARY EGGLESTON.

NEW YORK
G. P. PUTNAM'S SONS
27 AND 29 WEST 23D STREET

PREFACE.

In preparing this little book, I have done the work conscientiously, whether it shall prove to be well or ill done.

In every matter treated, I have given the advice I should give to a son or a brother—drawing my materials from every available source.

The narrow limits of the volume have compelled me to speak *ex cathedra* in many cases when I should have preferred to reverently cite authority, or to carefully state to the reader the premises from which my conclusions were drawn.

If I have spoken dogmatically, however, I would have the student remember that the whole spirit of my teaching is that he should never accept blindly the authority of any man or of any book, and to this rule my own little volume certainly does not claim to be an exception.

BROOKLYN, *September*, 1872.   G. C. E.

CONTENTS.

INTRODUCTION.

CHAPTER L .

HOW TO MARK OUT A COURSE OF STUDY.

CHAPTER II.

COMMON SCHOOL STUDIES.

CHAPTER III.

COLLEGIATE STUDIES.

CHAPTER IV.

THE STUDY OF LANGUAGES.

CHAPTER V.

THE HIGHER MATHEMATICS.

CHAPTER VI.

PHYSICAL SCIENCE.

CHAPTER VII.

MORAL AND INTELLECTUAL SCIENCE.

CHAPTER VIII.

GENERAL READING.

CONTENTS.

CHAPTER IX.

HOW TO STUDY AND READ TO THE BEST ADVANTAGE.

ERRATUM.

On p. 52, M. Marcel's work is said to be out of print. This, it appears, is not now the case, as the book is included in Messrs. D. Appleton & Co.'s Catalogue.

HOW TO EDUCATE YOURSELF.

INTRODUCTION.

THE NATURE AND PURPOSE OF THE BOOK.

LEST the purpose and meaning of this manual shall be misunderstood, let me say at the outset that I have no patent system of easy education to present. I can point out no "royal road to learning," for the reason that there is none, and in the very nature of things there never can be one.

And yet the sole purpose of this volume is to make the road to learning and culture somewhat easier than it is, particularly in the case of students who have no master.

Every educated man is, in some sense, self-educated. No teacher, whatever his abilities may be, can force an education upon an unwilling pupil. Furthermore, no teacher can educate a persistently idle pupil. He can bridge over difficulties ; he can point out the way ; he can advise and direct ; he can stimulate the student to activity ; but the real work must be done by the student himself, if it be done at all.

There is no denying the fact that regular teachers and regular schools are necessary to some students and

very valuable to all, and I have no sympathy whatever
with the prevalent cant which teaches that the men
commonly called " self-made " are greater, or better, or
wiser than those whose acquirements and culture have
been obtained through more regular channels. Dr.
Franklin was a wise man and an able one, and Mr.
Greeley has achieved a grand success in his profession.
Elihu Burritt learned a good deal about languages
while yet at the forge, and Robert Collyer has not forgotten how to make a horse-shoe while he has been
learning how to preach an eloquent sermon. But all
these men, and others like them, would have been even
more successful, or at any rate their success would
have come to them earlier in life, if they had had the
advantages of a regular training. The mistake commonly made is that of attributing their greatness to
their want of schooling, when in point of fact they are
great in spite of that want, because they have by untir-
ing industry supplied the defect, doing without teachers
that which they could have done much more easily and
much more perfectly with them. Hugh Miller wrought
out his knowledge of geology from the rocks in which
he worked as a craftsman ; but it does not follow that
the best road to geological lore lies through the business of a quarryman or a stonecutter.

Let no student delude himself with the idea that he
is above the need of instructors. If he can attend
good schools he should do so by all means, and his
education so acquired will be much more satisfactory,
much more perfectly rounded than it ever could be
otherwise.

But if attendance upon school instruction be impossible, or if the student be cut short in it, there is no oc-

casion for him to despair, or to abandon the work of educating himself. If he is to be educated at all, he must educate himself in any case, and while the task would be much easier in school than out, it is not impossible of accomplishment wholly without teachers.

The chief service which a teacher is called upon to render an earnest student, is that of guiding and directing his studies ; advising him what branches to pursue, and how to follow them with the best results. And herein lies the chief advantage which the earnest student in school has over the earnest student out of school. The one has his course marked out for him, and is instructed carefully in the readiest and surest means of mastering it. The other must mark out his own course, with such advice as he can get, and must pursue it after methods of his own devising, for the most part. Again, the one has, presumably, more time at his disposal, and better facilities every way, than the other, and therefore has less need to know how to economize his time closely in the selection and pursuit of his studies.

It is to cure precisely these defects that this book is, in the main, designed. My purpose is to supply, as far as possible, the place of a teacher to teacherless students, guiding them to a proper selection of subjects for study, and suggesting the best methods of pursuing each.

To this end I shall make free use of other people's experience, as well as my own, giving that which seems to me best, in every case, whether the idea be new or old, my own or some other person's. The plan of the book is a simple one. Each class of study will be examined as to its nature, its value, the peculiar advantages arising from the information contained in it, and from the culture it brings. Its difficulty, and all other circumstances bearing upon the student's selection, will be placed fairly before him, so that he may choose advisedly the branches to which he will give his attention.

After this, in each case, the best methods of pursuing the study will be given, together with such other hints, suggestions and warnings as every earnest and competent teacher finds frequent occasion to give.

In regard to reading and study outside of text-books, a similar plan will be pursued. I shall endeavor to guide the student in the selection of his literature by pointing out the nature and value of different classes of books, the kind of culture and the kind of information each gives, and to prepare him, as far as practicable, to make a judicious selection and arrangement of his reading matter for himself.

The book, as will be seen at a glance, is intended principally for students who must educate themselves outside of schools and colleges; but I am persuaded that even students whose advantages are of the best, will find many things to help them in these pages, and I write with the hope that my little book will supply to this class of students a kind of guidance of which I myself often felt the need both in school and at college.

A work of this kind must, in the nature of things, be very imperfect, because of the narrowness of its limits, if for no other reason; but having had frequent occasion to counsel and aid persons engaged in the work of self-education, I come to the task now, knowing pretty well the nature of the difficulties which beset this class of students. If the pages which follow shall be found to supply to them at all adequately the guidance and counsel they need, I shall be abundantly satisfied.

CHAPTER I.

HOW TO MARK OUT A COURSE OF STUDY.

WHAT TO STUDY.

THE first point to be decided in beginning every education is what to study. The student who can go to school and to college has the question answered for him, though not always wisely ; but he who must decide it for himself, is usually puzzled by the multiplicity of possible studies, and by his ignorance both of their character and of his own wants. And yet it is of the utmost importance that he should decide this question correctly. An error here is always serious, and sometimes the failure to master a badly-chosen subject leads to the abandonment of all effort in despair.

A COMMON ERROR.

It is a common error of people studying without a teacher to suppose that they must follow the course of the schools, taking not only every subject, but every text-book, in the order of school arrangement. To see the folly of this it is only necessary to remember that the student without a master has less time than the schoolboy to give to study, (else he might himself go

to school,) and that his progress will naturally be somewhat slower than that of the pupils for whom the
school course is intended, aided as they are by systematic instruction. Besides all this, there is a great deal
of time consumed in the schools over exercises that are
certainly not necessary or even useful to an earnest student, so resolved upon securing an education as to undertake it without the ordinary helps. This is due
partly perhaps to the fact that there are idle pupils in
every school whose first need is to be made active in
study, even if it be done by otherwise useless exercises ; but much more largely, doubtless, to the want of
judicious condensation in the text-books. The best-
cultivated men in America, for instance, unless their
avocations lead them to make geographical study a specialty, do not remember enough of their bulky, grad-
ed school text-books on the subject, to fill more than a
score of these pages. They remember all that is worth
remembering. They know all the leading facts, perhaps, but these might have been written in the smallest
of school-books and learned in a few weeks, while every
schoolboy plods for years through volume after volume
full of petty geographical details of no consequence in
themselves, never remembered, and certainly not worth
the learning to a young man who has his education to
get without assistance from others. And the same
thing is true in a greater or less degree of almost every
other branch of school study. The school course is intended for pupils who have time and opportunity to
master it. It has much that is almost wholly useless in
it, and it is certainly not suited, as a whole, to students
who must be their own teachers.

.

WHAT THEN, SHOULD BE THE STUDENT'S COURSE ?

Certainly not the same in every case ; hardly the same in any two cases. The question is one that must be decided with reference to the age, capacity and circumstances of each individual. The one who has hardly any leisure cannot master many things, and his slender list of studies should embrace only the ones most desirable for him to follow, while his fellow, whose leisure is more abundant, should make use of it in pursuing a wider course. It is very true that in all knowledge there is profit, but all knowledge is not equally profitable, and the man whose education must be a partial one at best, should aim to make it embrace such parts of the whole as will best serve the purposes of education in his particular case. And to enable us to ascertain what will do this, it is necessary that we shall inquire at the outset—

WHAT ARE THE PURPOSES OF EDUCATION ?

Different people have different ideas of life, and accordingly they pursue their studies with all kinds of ends in view. Men sometimes work pretty diligently over their books, with no higher motive than a desire to make a creditable appearance in society. Young people often have an ambition to appear learned with no great desire to be so, and so seek just enough of erudition to enable them to talk of things they know very little about, as if they understood them.

But education has two definite purposes to serve, and one or both of these should be in the mind of the student from first to last. The object most commonly

sought by the student is practical utility. He studies
because learning and the intellectual culture it brings
with it are things that have a market value ; because an
educated man can *make money* more readily and more
surely than an uneducated one can ; because his education will open up to him more agreeable business pursuits than an untaught man can follow.   To a certain
extent every man in this busy country of ours is in-
fluenced by these considerations.   We have no recognized aristocracy, and no entailed estates, and therefore
no man, among us, can be sure in advance that he will
never need to make his own way in the world.

With the people for whose benefit chiefly I write,
those who are compelled to educate themselves without
teachers, the practical utility of education is often of
course the main consideration ; but even these would do
well to keep before them the higher purpose of culture,
which is to fit the man for his most perfect work in life,
to make him, as nearly as his natural capacity will allow,
a completely cultured man, balanced, trained to the use
of all his faculties and able to command their highest
and best exercise at will.   That even people without
the advantages of academic training may accomplish
something like this is sufficiently seen in the fact that
the present editor of the *Atlantic Monthly*, a scholar, a
poet, an author and a critic, with certainly very few if
any superiors in America, in the matter of refined and
varied culture, left school to learn a trade at the age of
ten, and has never had a master since.

Everybody is not a Mr. Howells, however, and few
young men can hope to accomplish all that he has ; but
failing in that, it is well that the student shall feel the
high possibilities of his life and appreciate the nobler

purposes of his work. While he labors to fit himself
for his business, he will work none the less earnestly
for feeling that his study is making him more and
more the man nature intended that he should be.

THE COMPARATIVE VALUES OF VARIOUS STUDIES.

Whether the student contemplates a brief course or
an extended one, it is equally necessary for him to select his studies with reference first to their comparative
intrinsic values, and secondly with reference to their
comparative values to him individually. To do this intelligently he must bear in mind that there are two distinct uses of study. The first of these is the acquisition
of knowledge, and the second is intellectual training.

Each is good in its kind. Each has a practical value.
The man who knows arithmetic finds daily use for the
mere knowledge he has gained, in all the affairs of life.
But the value of the mental discipline he has received
in the study of arithmetic, while it may be less apparent, is no less real than the other. And this is true
too of every other branch of a well-ordered education.
Each is doubly useful. Each helps to train the mind
to proper action, and each furnishes some knowledge
which is of use in itself. But all are not equally valuable in either of these ways, and the proportion of time
and attention to be given to each should be regulated
with reference to their comparative importance.

HERBERT SPENCER'S CLASSIFICATION.

Mr. Herbert Spencer, in his work on education, has
attempted to make an elaborate classification of the various subjects of study, and to arrange them in the order

of their relative comparative importance, a task that he is as well qualified as anybody else, perhaps, to perform, but one in which even he has only partially succeeded. Such a classification in a manual like this, intended mainly for students without masters, would be manifestly impracticable, and hence nothing of the kind is attempted. I prefer to offer some plain suggestions which will aid the student to ascertain for himself just what he wants.

THE FACTORS INVOLVED.

In the first place, then, it is necessary to take into account your age and whatever other circumstances there may be which tend to limit you in point of time.

If you are already grown, with the cares of business about you, your time for self-education is necessarily very limited, and your selection of studies must of course be made with reference to this fact, so that you may not spend any portion of your scanty leisure upon that which is not absolutely essential. Take an inventory of the time at your disposal, as you would of your capital before entering upon business, in order that you may invest it wisely.

It is next necessary to ask yourself what your practical necessities are in the matter of learning ; what your business in life is, or is to be ; what information you will especially need in that business, and what studies will give you the necessary knowledge. And this is clearly a point worthy of attention in any case, whether the education is to be abundant or scanty. To the man who intends to make himself a physician, for instance, a knowledge of chemistry is of prime importance, while the higher mathematics furnish him very little of

any immediate value. To the one who would be an en·
gineer, on the other hand, mathematics is the one thing
especially needful. I am speaking now with reference
solely to the value of the information gained in these
studies, and not of their value as intellectual exercises.
Decide then, secondly, what you want in the matter of
learning—what studies will give you the information
you most need for the accomplishment of your ends,
whatever these may be.

The third point to be determined in settling upon a
course of study is more difficult, and in the very nature
of things can never be very accurately decided in the beginning by the student himself. Simply stated, the
question is, " What mental discipline do I need ?" and
it is one which should recur at every step of the student's progress. It is one which every cultivated man
asks himself constantly. It governs the already accomplished scholar in the selection of his books for reading
even more than it influences the student in marking out
his course of study, and it can never be wholly determined in advance. Just here comes in the higher purpose of education, the making of a well-balanced man.
It is the training of all the faculties to their fullest capacity, the development of all the forces, the just subjection of each to the whole, that fits the man for his most
perfect work, and most completely fulfills the purpose
of education; and the nearer we come to this ideal con-
dition of perfect and symmetrical development, in body,
mind and morals, the better are we prepared for the
successful pursuit of our especial businesses in life.

But aside from this, in nearly every profession and
trade there exists a necessity for mental discipline in
specific directions. A special intellectual development

is of practical value, just as the possession of a particular kind of information is, and to this extent the especial needs of the student in the matter of intellectual culture as a preparation for a specific business career may be decided in advance with tolerable accuracy. In a large degree, indeed, the culture made necessary by merely economic considerations depends upon the character of the student himself. If he be of dreamy mood, visionary, absent, lacking control of his intellectual operations, the mathematics and the physical sciences will tend of course to correct the fault, and will have a value to him which they would otherwise lack. And so with every other branch of study. Each may serve to correct some intellectual fault, to supply an intellectual want, or to strengthen the man in a point of weakness. And in deciding what and how much to study, reference must of course be had to the peculiar intellectual needs that are to be supplied. Let the student, then, after he has taken a fair inventory of the time at his disposal, ask himself—

1st. *What knowledge do I most need?*

2nd. *What culture do I most need?*

And when he shall have answered these questions, his way will be clear to the marking out of a course of study suited to his especial case.

But let him remember that in all knowledge there is profit, and that the wider his culture is, the more nearly he will come to the perfection of manhood at which he should aim, the better prepared he will be to do his best work.   While he must consider first his actual and immediate educational wants, he should never lose sight of the fact that the course of study he has marked out for himself will supply these but imper fectly, and that other knowledge and other culture are desirable, not only in a general way, but also as bearing directly upon his success in life. With this in view he will find abundant opportunity, while pursuing his prescribed course of study and reading, to widen it somewhat at times; and by some of the modes of economizing time and labor suggested elsewhere in this volume, he may almost certainly enlarge the range of both the information and the culture he has prescribed for himself.

For the sake of convenience let me briefly sum up the spirit of what I have said thus far, in direct sentences :

Take an inventory of the time at your disposal, that you may know how much you can study.

Do not attempt too much, lest you become discouraged and fail altogether.

On the other hand, remember that within the limits imposed by your circumstances, the more you shall master the better educated you will be.

Select your studies with reference first to the value of the learning they will give you, and secondly to the value of the culture their mastery will bring.

Give the preference to those branches which will tend most directly to fit you for your special business, but enlarge your culture and information as opportunity shall offer.

Such are the general principles that should guide the student in marking out his course of study, and to a large extent each must apply them for himself ; but some more specific directions may be of service, and in fulfillment of my design to make this manual as largely useful as possible, I give them in their proper places.

CHAPTER II.

THE WASTE OF TIME.

IT is a singular fact, perhaps, but a fact nevertheless which everybody except the teachers themselves recognizes, that there is a larger proportion of useless work expended in the common schools than anywhere else. Many of the branches taught there are wholly useless in themselves, and nearly all the others are so overloaded with unimportant details that the pupil loses sight of their real purpose and quits them at last, wearied with misspent labor, having gained but little of the information or culture they should have brought him.

OF GEOGRAPHY

I have already spoken. Pupils spend years in studying text-books not one tenth part of which is worth learning, while not one twentieth of their contents is ever remembered. As soon as the examinations are over the student begins to forget—forgetting much more rapidly than he learned—and in forgetting, he sometimes loses the useful with the useless parts.

Clearly there is too much geography taught. The books are too large and too numerous. They have altogether too many details in them, and moreover, no book whatever is necessary to the learning of all that anybody except a professional geographer or a navigator needs to know of geography. A brief examination of the globes and a few weeks' earnest study of good maps will serve to give the student a fair general knowledge of geography, and this is all that anybody not professionally pursuing geographical studies ever remembers or needs to remember. Reference to a map is always readily made when fuller information on any particular point is wanted, just as reference to a dictionary or encyclopædia is, and to attempt to learn and remember all the facts of geography in detail is almost as absurd as it would be to commit an unabridged dictionary to memory as an introduction to English.

HOW TO STUDY GEOGRAPHY.

I say, therefore, to the student without a master, waste no time in the study of geographies. Learn the general outlines and relative localities of seas and continents by examining the globe, and then give yourself to a progressive study of maps until you are familiar with the chief facts of geography—that is to say, till you know the relative localities and the general outlines of all the countries, the nationality and general features of the chief rivers, ranges of mountains, etc., and the places of the world's great cities, etc., on the maps.

Take first a general map of each continent ; then one of each country ; and finish your study of the subject by a careful scrutiny of the State and local maps of your own country. When you shall have done this you will have a good general knowledge of geography, and very few people have more than this, or need more. An occasional reference to good maps, afterwards will perserve and greatly add to the information thus gained.

ARITHMETIC,

of course, everybody needs to know, and it cannot be learned too thoroughly. But in the ordinary way of teaching and learning it, a good deal of time is wasted, and the best results are rarely secured. There is a good deal of unnecessary matter in the text-books, and that which is necessary is too often so put as to lead the student to lose sight of its proper purpose, and thus lose the advantage he should gain from its study.

Let the student bear in mind from first to last that everything in Mathematics is *fact ;* that every fact there has been *discovered* and nothing invented.   Let him remember that what are commonly called rules are not rules at all, but that each is merely a statement of one of the ways in which certain principles may be applied to the solution of certain classes of problems, and that more than one of these principles may be used in almost every case.   Let me explain this a little more at length.   The student finds many pages devoted to common fractions, and a like number to decimals.   Under each head is arranged a number of problems, together with a rule for working them.   By all the arrangements made for him, by the classifications of the book, by the traditions of the schoolroom, and by every other direct and indirect means, he is forced to the conclusion that some of these problems are of a kind to be solved by the one rule, while the others are of a totally different character and can be wrought only upon the other principle.   Of course any teacher, upon

being questioned, would tell a student that this is not
the case ; but there is really nothing in the ordinary way
of learning and teaching arithmetic to suggest such
questioning, and, with one remarkable exception, I
have never known a teacher who thought it necessary
or desirable to explain the point without waiting for
accident to suggest inquiry   I would have the student
remember constantly that Addition, Subtraction, Multiplication and Division, are the only fundamental rules of
arithmetic, and that all the others are but applications
of these.   He should bear in mind also that the various
problems given may each be solved in more than one
way—that their solution is not the object of his study ;
that their solution is not a matter of any importance
whatever, except as it exercises him in the application
of the principles involved and verifies the correctness
and accuracy of his understanding.   With these points
established in his mind, let him go to work to learn
each of the principles involved,—that is to say, let him
pass nothing that he does not fully understand, let him
accept nothing as true until he fully understands the
fact that it is true, and the reason why it is true ; or, if
he must pass it, let him refer to it again and again until
he does understand it.   He will then need no rules, and
will not be dependent, in after life, upon a fallacious
memory for rules, which, even if remembered correctly,
might readily be misapplied by one who had failed to
master the principles involved.

Teachers sometimes tell pupils all this, and some of
them succeed in impressing the fact upon the minds
of those under their tuition, but in altogether too many
cases their system of teaching makes it easy for the
parrot pupil to make a better show than the one who

labors over principles, and thus there is an immediate
and constant temptation before every pupil to do that
which the teacher is continually cautioning him
not to do. On the other hand there are teachers whose
indolence or incompetence leads them to omit even
the verbal caution, while the student without a master stands in especial need of the warning.

I remember a schoolfellow of my own who went
with me through the arithmetic, solved every problem,
knew every rule, and was regarded as fellow of the
best of us. His practice was to commit each rule to
memory, and to follow it clause by clause in the working of every problem under it. He passed good examinations, of course, and afterwards graduated well in a
commercial college. I happened to be with him ten
years later, when he was attempting to fill the post of
bill clerk in a commission house. His calculations for
several days went unchallenged, as the bookkeeper
was overburdened with other duties and supposed him
competent. Before his first week ended, however, he
came hurriedly from his desk to ask confidentially
about a point in his practical arithmetic. He had to
calculate the total value of a given number of bushels
of corn at $1.08 per bushel. He had set the figures
down in the ordinary way, had multiplied by the eight,
and now *wanted to know what to do with the nought!*
Of course in school, while his " rules " were fresh in his
mind, no such difficulty had bothered him ; but now,
remembering no verbal rule for the case, he was unable
to work this simple problem in multiplication. The
case is an extreme one, doubtless, but it serves to illus
trate the importance of the precept I am endeavoring
to impress upon the reader. I would have him under-

stand each operation as he makes it—comprehend each principle before he undertakes to use it, and know why he does each thing as soon as he learns that he is to do it.   To do this by means of books only is often difficult.   The principles are all explained, of course, in every good arithmetic, but the explanations are not always sufficiently lucid, and the student often falls into the delusion of thinking that he understands a matter because he can repeat the explanation, even when this explanation is by no means clear to his comprehension. To remedy this there is nothing so good as a resort to object lessons.   I have had occasion to explain difficulties of this class to a good many pupils, many of them advanced far beyond the point where the difficulty occurred, and I have found a resort to the simplest forms of numbers, and an explanation by means of actual, tangible objects, far better than anything else possible.

In one instance, I remember, a bright, keen-witted girl who was studying algebra came to me for assistance.   I explained the problem in hand so that she could work it readily, but I saw that she only dimly comprehended my most labored explanations of the principles involved, and I was not satisfied with this. I questioned her to ascertain where her difficulty lay, and was led presently to ask her :

" Do you understand the multiplication and division of fractions ?"

" Algebraic fractions ?" she asked.

" Fractions of any kind," said I.   " Do you know, for instance, why the division of any quantity by a fraction gives a result larger than the dividend ?"

" No," she said, she had never been able to understand that, and although she had gone conscientiously through the arithmetic to the entire satisfaction of her teachers, she had never felt that she understood the principles involved in the working of fractions.

I took a score of apples, and undertook to teach her in a single lesson what years of schooling had left untaught.

I showed her how every reduction in the size of the divisor increased the result. Going downward gradually, I reached one as the divisor, which gave, of course, just twice as large a result as two had given. Then with a knife I made halves of the apples, and taking one of these in my hand, as a divisor, I was about to continue the explanation, when she fairly clapped her hands for joy. She saw the principle and understood now not only this, but every other fact she had learned concerning fractions, because she now knew practically just what fractions were. She at once adopted the plan with herself, and she has mastered the higher mathematics without a teacher, and almost without a serious difficulty.

I give the incident because it illustrates what I mean, shows the value of object-teaching, and may serve to guide some teacherless student in making use of objects in working out his own lessons.*

The student who thus masters every principle as he goes on will make slow progress, perhaps, at first, but in doing this he is laying a foundation for much more rapid as well as much more satisfactory learning after a little while. As soon as he clearly sees what figures mean,

---

* Of course nobody will imagine for a moment that I put this plan forward as in any sense new. It is only part of the great system of object-teaching known to every intelligent instructor, but used far less generally than it should be.

and learns to associate them with their meanings, mathematics loses its abstract character, its study becomes an agreeable one, and the relations of numbers to each other become clear, unmistakable facts to his mind, which he has no difficulty in comprehending. And this relation of numbers to each other is all there is of arithmetic.

Let me add one suggestion which I have found of value in a great many cases. There is nothing so good as *concrete* study, and the student of arithmetic should make an exercise out of every combination of numbers he can get outside of his arithmetic. When he reads in a newspaper, for instance, that there were two hundred and fifty-six persons on board a wrecked vessel, of whom twenty-eight were drowned and eight died of exposure, he has an excellent exercise in the calculation of the various percentages involved. And so with a hundred other things. Excellent problems may be made out of the dimensions of every room in the house, out of every planted field, out of everything in fact around the student, and these may be made to involve precisely the principles he most wishes to study, whether they be those of arithmetic or those of the higher mathematics.

They have the advantage too of being real, practical problems, involving tangible facts, and there is no better way of making one's self a perfect master of arithmetic than by the persistent use of these every-day object-lessons with which we are all surrounded. Let the student practice making them for himself, and he will find no lack of material for his purpose.

Under another title in this volume I shall endeavor to show how a somewhat similar process may be made to contribute very largely to the student's progress in things other than arithmetic, and to enlarge his culture even more rapidly than the regular study of books can do.

We come now to

THE STUDY OF ENGLISH.

As our own language is the vehicle through which we communicate our thoughts to others and receive their ideas in return, of course every American needs to know English thoroughly. Looking at the matter from the lowest plane it is easy enough to see that a mastery of English has a decided pecuniary value to its possessor. In large commercial houses the accomplished English scholar who sits at the correspondent's desk usually receives double the salary paid to the much harder-worked bookkeeper, in spite of the fact that the latter brings to the business the capital of a technical skill. And there are scores of other ways in which a thorough knowledge of one's mother tongue may be made to pay, while its absence is often fatal to success. An ill-spelled letter, an ungrammatical remark—these and similar things have cost many a failure.

The money value of English study is by no means small, but aside from this, there can be no question of the fact that the study of English, properly followed, brings with it nearly, if not quite, as much of intellectual culture as the study of any other language, and with these facts in view, I think there can be no doubt that next to elementary arithmetic there is nothing more important in a common school education than the study of English. And yet it seems singularly neglected. Not one in fifty, even of classically educated men, can write a single page in perfectly accurate English. This may appear to be an extravagant statement, but I make it after a careful examination of results, and am convinced that it by no means goes beyond the fact. A great many cannot even write in tolerably good English, while the number of people who can spell correctly is so small that I have known more than one person to argue that the ability to spell is "a gift,"—that it comes, as high musical attainments do, only to those who have especial intellectual endowments in that direction. The absurdity of such a theory is too manifest to need demonstration. A memory which receives and retains the ten thousand occurrences of every day life is certainly equal to the task of remembering the order of letters in our constantly used words, particularly as the sound actively aids the memory in this matter, as it does not in ordinary affairs.

THE FAILURE OF THE GRAMMARS.

A thorough and accurate knowledge of English is of very great value to all. But while I think it impossible to attach too much importance to the study of English, I do not regard our grammars, as they are written, as of much use in any case, while to a great many people they are simply stumbling-blocks. Mr. Richard Grant White has shown, and most thinking people had already discovered, that our whole system of conjugating verbs after the manner of the Latin language is an absurdity; that "I might have been loved" is no more a part of the verb "to love" than is any other phrase in which "love" or "loved" occurs. Our language is almost wholly without verbal inflections, and the translation of a Latin verb in its different moods and tenses into English phrases of the same meaning, certainly does not give moods and tenses in English. Indeed, the grammarians have been singularly inconsistent in this. If the English phrase by which we express the thing that the Romans meant when they used the first person, singular number, subjunctive mood, future perfect tense of the verb "Amo" is properly called, in English, a like inflection of the verb "to love," then the same rule should apply to nouns, adjectives, etc., and we should have the word "man" declined, in English, as follows :

Nominative,	A man.
Genitive,	Of a man.
Dative,	To or for a man.
Accusative,	A man.
Vocative,	O man.
Ablative,	With, from, in, or by a man.

But we have nothing of the sort in any of the grammars. Our grammarians have translated the Latin verbs into English phrases and named these after the inflections of which they have the force, while they wholly omit to do the same thing with the nouns.

This is but one of many absurdities, which this is not the place to point out, and I have only given a single illustration for the sake of suggesting rather than explaining to the reader, my reasons for saying that while I regard the study of English *grammar* as of the utmost importance, I think the study of English *grammars* almost wholly useless in all cases, and actually hurtful in many.

Let it be understood, then, that what the student wants is to study English *grammar* whether he studies

English *grammars* or not. I would have him learn the structure, the philosophy, the origin, and the use of his mother tongue, and I am convinced that there are better ways of doing this than the one ordinarily adopted, in the chewing of dry husks at the bidding of a grammarian who defines an adverb to be "a word which qualifies or limits a verb, adjective, or other adverb," and then proceeds to tell the pupil that the word "yes" is an adverb, in spite of the fact that no sentence can possibly be formed in which this word will in any way qualify or limit anything whatever. The ordinary system of studying English is slow, irksome, and productive of poor results in the great majority of cases. That there is a much better way I am fully convinced, and it is one of the purposes of this chapter to explain to the student what this better way is.

The English grammars very correctly define English grammar to be "the art of speaking and writing the English language correctly," though they proceed to treat of many things in no way embraced in this definition, while they omit many of the essentials to such an art.

HOW TO STUDY GRAMMAR.

Discarding their system and accepting their definition, we find that in order to speak and write the English language correctly, it is necessary to know

1*st*. How to pronounce the words ;

2*nd*. How to spell the words ;

3*rd*. What the words mean ;

4*th*. How to frame them into correct sentences.

PRONUNCIATION.

We learn the correct pronunciation of most words as we learn the words themselves, by hearing others use them. Analogy gives us the sound of many others, and for the rest, errors are corrected and doubts easily solved by reference to the dictionaries.

SPELLING.

It cannot be denied that the orthography of our language is a difficult one. It follows few analogies, it has many redundancies, it is often awkward, and in a general way, there are no principles governing it. Some attempts have been made to frame rules for spelling, but these for the most part are of small value, covering but a meagre list of words, and admitting of many exceptions. There are but two of them that I have found of practical value to anybody. One of these is that monosyllables and words accented on the last syllable, ending in a single consonant, preceded by a single vowel, double the final consonant before an addition beginning with a vowel. It is a long rule, covering a very short list of words. It may enable a student to avoid spelling such words as " beginning," " plotting," " shipping," etc., with a single " n," " t," or " p," but beyond this it is of no service whatever. The other rule to which I refer is that the diphthong " ei " usually follows " c," while its companion, " ie," is generally used after other consonants ; for example, in the words " receive," " deceive," " perceive," etc., the " e " takes precedence, while the " i " comes first in such words as " field," " shield," " believe," " relieve," " chief," " thief," etc. This rule serves a good purpose, inasmuch as it meets a very common difficulty, but there are a good many exceptions to it, and they greatly lessen its value.

As these are the best of the rules given in any of the grammars, and the best that can be given, it will be seen at once that English spelling must be learned to a great extent arbitrarily, but a little industry and attention will enable any student to master it.

To a very great extent we *absorb* a knowledge of spelling in our daily reading. The original process of learning to read is itself a learning to spell, and as we read words correctly spelled in our newspapers and books, we naturally fall into the way of spelling most of them aright. Every person who reads must learn to spell at least half the words in our commonly used vocabulary. This far we are all able to spell, but there is no reason why any student should habitually spell any considerable number of words badly ; no reason, at any rate, except that the system by which spelling is commonly taught is an essentially bad one. Everybody knows what that system is, and everybody knows too how imperfectly it accomplishes its purpose. It is like all other parrot-teaching, in that its results are rapidly lost as soon as the attention is given to something else.

Experience and observation have combined to convince me that no person can be taught to spell, but that any person may learn to spell. In other words, I am convinced that no teacher of spelling is either necessary or useful to persons who can read and write. If the student would learn to spell words, let him use words. Let him write every day, and in writing, whenever he shall come to a word which he does not certainly know how to spell, let him look for it in his dictionary, examining its derivation as well as its spelling. Then let him look also at all the words derived from it, and when this is done he will never hesitate again as to the orthography of any of them.

To do this as an exercise is easy enough of course, but when one is writing for other purposes he is apt to find it more convenient to ask some one else how to spell the word, or even to guess at it, than to go to his dictionary ; and just here is the common point of failure. A spelling so arbitrary as ours is can only be mastered by industry, and the student who has not industry enough to examine the dictionary for himself in every case, has no right to hope for anything like complete success. I cannot too strongly impress the student with the necessity of holding himself strictly to this rule. It may consume valuable time at first, but the occasions for going to the dictionary will rapidly diminish in frequency under a faithful following of the plan suggested, and the results will fully compensate him for all the trouble taken.

Inattention is a fruitful source of ill spelling. I mean by this not merely that in moments of inattention we are apt to spell incorrectly words that we know how to spell, but also that by inattention the student loses many opportunities of learning the orthography of words for the first time. I can best explain this by a few examples of the simplest kind. I have seen the word "preparation" spelled with an "e" in the second syllable, simply because the writer failed to remember that "preparation" is a derivation of "prepare." Hardly a day passes in which I do not see "separate" or some of its derivatives similarly misspelled by people who know Latin reasonably well, and know that the Latin word from which our "separate" comes is a compound one, made up of " se " and " parare." A very little measure of attention would show them the absolute necessity there is for an " a " in the second syllable, and yet I find an " e " there in eleven out of sixteen instances now before me, all of them taken from the manuscript of educated men, who could give the derivation of the word without a moment's hesitation. These are but two cases cited here by way of illustration. Scores of others might easily be added, but my purpose now is simply to suggest the way in which a little care and attention may be made to serve the student in learning to spell accurately.

LEARNING THE MEANINGS OF WORDS.

In some sort we absorb a knowledge of the meanings of words, but the popular use of words is by no means always a very accurate one, and the nicer distinctions which constitute at once the beauty and the power of language are often wholly lost in our common speech. A good knowledge of these is of the first importance to the student who aspires to become anything like a good English scholar. For the accomplishment of this, methods very similar to those I have indicated for use in learning to spell will be found indispensable. Whenever the student hears, sees or uses a word of which he does not know the full and precise meaning, with its synonyms and their departures from absolute synonymy, he should at once make the word a study, examining his dictionary carefully for all the information there given on the subject, and comparing the word with its synonyms for the sake of learning the peculiarities of each, and the purpose each serves in our speech. The amount and variety of information to

be acquired in this way is very much greater than most
students will imagine, and there is no better or more
rapid way of learning English than precisely this. But
to do this worthily will require a good deal of industry,
and it may even cause some inconvenience at times. Indolence and self-indulgence are greatly in the way in this
as in all other attempts to learn anything thoroughly.

In thus studying the spelling and the meaning of
words, the student will find it an excellent plan to carry
a memorandum-book in which to write down, when a
dictionary is not at hand, words of which he wishes to
make studies.

In the study of meanings, too, a little attention to
the forms, kinships, derivations, etc., of the words will
be found of quite as great assistance as a similar process is in the matter of spelling. This is especially the
case with people who know anything of Latin, Greek,
French or Anglo-Saxon, because to such persons a
large number of our English words bear their meaning
on their faces, if only the student takes care to look for
it. But even people who know nothing of any language except their own will find in many words traces
of their origin, from which all their nicer shades of
meaning are at once apparent. Aside from the time
saved by this process when it is applicable, it has the
greater merit of supplying a much more thorough and
accurate knowledge of the words and their uses that
any study of mere definitions can give.

It would seem at the first glance that this habit of
analytical attention to the formation of words, would
so commend itself to every one as to need no mention
here, but I am convinced that the fact is otherwise. I
have known many good Latin scholars to habitually

use the word "transpire" as the equivalent of "happen," and certainly no one familiar with Latin could possibly fall into such an error, except with eyes shut to the transparent formation of the word so misused. And the same thing happens every day with hundreds of other words, that express their meaning in the very syllables and letters of which they are composed, and yet are constantly misused by people who ought to know better, and do know better, if they would only trouble themselves to think of the matter.

THE STRUCTURE OF SENTENCES.

Words, taken separately, are of no value. They are but the bricks out of which the building, language, is constructed, and we no sooner begin to learn their meanings than we begin also to learn how to put them together into intelligible sentences. We learn this in a rude way, just as we learn approximate meanings, by absorption from the people around us. As we grow older our reading greatly increases our information on this subject, at the same time correcting many of the errors adopted from oral speech. But to learn the genius of the language, to master its idiom, to comprehend its principles, and to acquire so thorough a mastery over it as to make it a soft clay in our hands which we can mould as we will to our uses, are ends that can be accomplished only by long and earnest work.

Let us look a little into the processes. In the grammars we have the dry husks of syntax, simple enough, and even tolerably interesting to people who have already learned all that these are intended to teach, but quite useless and almost wholly unintelligible to the student seeking to learn these things. The grammars tell of moods and tenses, with names that are anything but indicative to the boys and girls who are expected to use them. Then follow "rules," varying in number according to the fancy of the grammarian—rules like those in the arithmetics, that are simply statements of facts, that teach no principles, and are of no manner of use, except in the solution of the syntactical problems arrayed under them as exercises. Doubtless some people have learned English from these grammars, but in the main their use is certainly of questionable advantage. Dull pupils cannot comprehend them; bright ones get on better, in the study of English, without them.

There is no better way of learning the structure of any complicated thing than by taking it to pieces and putting it together again, and there is no better way of learning the English language, certainly. Indeed, the writers of the ordinary grammars recognize this fact, and their whole effort is to instruct and practice the student in doing just this. But I think with Mr. White, and a good many other lovers of idiomatic English, that our grammarians have been misled by the old scholastic influences into an attempt to make our speech conform to the Latin, and so have built upon it • an unphilosophical system of inflections, and encumbered it with a set of rules that have no root in the nature of the language itself. The limitations of this manual would not admit of the discussion of this subject here, even if the view I take had not been already ably maintained by the author to whose work I have referred.

But while I do not think any ordinary grammar necessary or very useful to the student who has no master, there are text-books on English gram-

mar which will aid him greatly in his study of the language. Such a book as Greene's Analysis, for instance, in which parts of speech, and conjugations and
rules of syntax, and all the cumbrous technicalities of
grammars are wholly done away with, while the author
leads the student step by step from the simplest to the
most complex of sentences, analyzing them and showing the student the nature and office of every part, will
be found invaluable. There are several text-books of
the sort, in which the English language is treated phi-
losophically and rationally, with but few technicalities ;
but the one named is one of the best for the self-teaching student, in that it is one of the simplest.

But just here it is well to remind the reader that the
book, even if it shall be thoroughly mastered, will not
teach him English. As he studies its pages he should
form the habit of going outside of them and questioning
the sentences he reads elsewhere for confirmation and illustration of the text. He should make exercises every
day of the books or papers within his reach, and of the
remarks made in his presence. This will serve not only
to fasten in his mind the principles laid down in the
text, but also to show him the departures from them
that are common in conversation, and he will soon learn
to know which of these are errors to be avoided at all
times, and which are simply conversational idioms, ad-
missible as such, but not authorized for other purposes.

HIGHER ENGLISH.

From the Analysis, and from this daily application of
its teachings, the student will learn the laws governing
the language.

Having faithfully followed the system of study indicated, he will now have learned how to pronounce the words; how to spell the words; what the words mean · and how to put them together into sentences. In other words he will know how to speak and write the English language correctly. He will have learned the grammar of our tongue.

But many people can speak and write the language correctly who cannot speak or write it well. Many people who never use an incorrect sentence, never frame a graceful one. Correct English may be, and often is very stiff English, and the student who has gone this far is by no means master of the language as yet. He has still to learn how to write and speak in graceful sentences, and how to handle the tongue deftly, as an infinitely flexible instrument, completely under his control.

Such a mastery over English is acquired, of course, by very few people, comparatively, but the end is one so worthy that the student should spare no effort to accomplish it as fully as possible, and every approach to it is a step in the direction of ripe scholarship of the very best sort.

The means that have been employed to this end are various, and almost every student will be able to add to my suggestions many valuable exercises of his own. Indeed these self-devised lessons are often the very best ones possible for the student, inasmuch as they commonly spring from a known and felt necessity of his own, and therefore supply the wants of his peculiar temperament and circumstances much more directly than any exercise suggested by others can possibly do. I shall confine myself therefore to the recommendation of plans which I have known to work well, urging the

student to vary them whenever he finds that a change
will better adapt them to his own particular case.

An approved text-book on English composition will
supply a good deal of needed information, while it will
furnish also the rules governing good English speech,
and guide the student in the correction of inelegances
of phrase. (Dr. John S. Hart's very admirable series of
text-books are probably the best, especially for self-
instructed students.) No text-book on the subject aims
to do more than this, and indeed none can do more.
The rest must be learned from extensive reading, or by
means of exercises, and these, as I have said, may be
varied almost at will. The one most commonly employed in the schools is composition-writing, and this,
with a competent teacher as critic, is ordinarily found
to be extremely valuable.

Even without criticism the practice of telling things
in writing will bring with it a certain degree of fluency
and ease in the use of language, and every student of
English should write something every day. If the
thing that he writes shall prove not to be a composition,
in the school-room sense of the term, it will be so much
the better, simply because in real life people talk very
little about abstract matters, while it is only the thoroughly earnest and thoroughly practical teacher who
succeeds in making his composition-writers treat of anything else.

Let the student who would master English, then,
write something every day. If he simply tells a homely
anecdote, or relates the incidents of the day, or gives
an account of something he has seen, to an imaginary
circle of readers, or if he writes down what he has
thought upon any subject, the result will probably be

worth nothing in a literary way, but its writer will have had an excellent lesson in English.

There is another admirable exercise, closely akin to this. It was technically known in the High School where it originated as " narration ;" certain pupils were named, each day, as the narrators for the following day, and each was required to take the rostrum and tell something to the school. They were allowed to tell anything they chose, but always in their own words, and the rapidity with which the pupils improved in their manner of saying what they had to say, not only on the rostrum but equally in other places, was very marked. The student without a school may quietly exercise himself in a similar way in the company of his fellows without letting anybody into his secret. An audience is an audience, whether its members are aware of the fact or not.

Another excellent plan is to take sentences from books, or elsewhere, and practice expressing their ideas in a variety of other forms. It is best to take single sentences at first, and to see in how many ways you can express the same ideas, using the same words or others as convenience may dictate. Then take two or three sentences on a single subject and repeat the process, practicing also the expression of the ideas contained in your two or three sentences, in a single, compound, or complex sentence. Reversing the process, take a long compound or complex sentence, and break it up into a number of simple ones, fully expressing the same idea.

This much may be done mentally, when the materials for writing are not at hand, when the student is at work, or when he is walking, or riding, or doing anything else that does not require his constant attention, in pursuance of the habit of thought-education suggested elsewhere in this volume.

When you shall have acquired a good degree of facility in this exercise, a somewhat more elaborate application of the princlpie will be found of very great advantage. Read a very short article of any kind, and then turning away from it write down its substance in your own way, or still better, in three or four different ways, taking care to preserve the precise meaning of the original, and to omit nothing. At first this will be done awkwardly, but after a little practice you will find it easy to say the same thing in half a dozen different ways, and when you can do this the flexibility of the language in your hands will be greatly increased. When you shall find this to be the case, follow the plan with longer articles, taking care all the time not to make use of awkward, confused, or very complex sentences. Remember that of two ways of expressing precisely the same thing, the simpler one is always the better.

Just here, let me give a word of caution. If the student has read any of the books upon English composition, he is in danger of falling into troublesome errors by too strict an adherence to the rules they lay down. Let him bear in mind, constantly, that these rules are only general ones, and are not applicable in every case. They are framed, for the most part, for the correction of those errors into which very young writers commonly fall, and while they are necessary for this purpose, even their authors do not intend that they should have a wider application than this.

Let me illustrate this. One of these rules is to the

effect that tautological expressions are bad, and in a general way this is very true ; but there are cases in which the frequent repetition of the same word or the same idea greatly adds to the force of writing, and a strict application of the rule in such cases as these, is of course not intended. Again, there is a very simple rule, that where several substantives are coupled toge ther, either as the subject or the object of the verb, the conjunction "and" or "or" must be used only between the last two. For example, "Men, women, children, horses and dogs, joined in the chase," is better than "Men and women and children" etc., and ordinarily the rule holds good in this way. There are times, however, when it is better to write all the conjunctions, and our very best writers frequently do so.

To decide when it is better to adhere to these and similar rules, and when it is better to depart from them, is the office of taste, and good taste in literary matters comes only from careful culture. I can give the student no clue to the problem—no formula by which he can solve it, but I have given this caution in order that the reader who begins with a proper respect for rule may also cultivate, from the first, a reasonable independence of rule, in order that the guides given him in his text-books may not become his prison-keepers, as they are very apt to do with students who have no other masters. What I would press upon him is briefly this, that the rules given him in the text-books on composition and rhetoric are in the main correct, but that not one of them is applicable always and everywhere. In avoiding the errors they are designed to correct, beware of falling into errors of an opposite kind. Let your taste and your judgment be educated by these rules, but never allow either to be arbitrarily controlled by them. Apply the rules when they are applicable, but hold yourself free to depart from their strict letter whenever it carries a meaning contrary to their spirit. They are meant to be guide-boards, and not impassable barriers to the student. He should catch their spirit, taking care to ascertain just what they are intended to teach, and just what errors they are designed to prevent, keeping constantly in mind the fact that except in the matter of grammatical accuracy, there can be no rule of universal application on the subject of English composition. I have found no greater stumbling-block in the way of self-teaching students than the habit of blindly following rules that were never meant to be so followed.

There is another exercise in English composition which helps to give the student freedom in the use of language, while its practice teaches him something else at the same time. It is to read brief editorial comments on current events, and to write something quite different upon the same subjects and from the same facts. This is what is known in newspaper offices as paragraphing, and every editor knows how very few people do it thoroughly well. While it forms an excellent exercise in the use of English, it serves at the same time to sharpen the wits and to cultivate a habit of independent thinking which is absolutely essential to all profitable reading. The man who reads books as gospels, accepting their statements of fact and their conclusions as necessarily true, becomes the mere creature of his books, and his ideas are but reflections, and often faint ones at that, of other people's thoughts. He has his opinions at second-hand, and they are worth little to himself and still less to anybody else. His mind is a lumber-room. He has succeeded in getting some learning, perhaps, but it has brought with it no culture. Against a habit with tendencies of this kind we cannot take too many precautions, and the exercise just suggested furnishes a most admirable training in habits of reading the very opposite of the unfortunately common one to which I refer.

But as a means of culture in English, the constant reading of good authors is more effective than anything else, and upon that, chiefly, the student must depend for excellence in this as in a good many other departments of learning and culture.

A rather remarkable case, illustrating the effectiveness of reading as a teacher of English, was that of George Northrup, the trapper. His education was extremely limited ; his opportunities for intercourse with men of culture were very few, and his habits of life as a trapper were certainly not of a kind to supply educational defects. But he was a constant reader of De Quincey, Irving, and Bancroft, and when he wrote newspaper letters from the Indian wars, the purity and grace of his literary style were the wonder of everybody who knew the history of the man.

CHAPTER III.

WHAT TO STUDY.

In planning this volume I have had the one purpose of making it as generally useful as possible, constantly in view. To this end I make my chapters and other subdivisions with reference rather to the convenience of students than to any strictly philosophical system of classification. I have called the branches already treated, Common School Studies, not because they are fully taught in the average common school, but because they ought to be. In like manner I include under the title "Collegiate Studies" all that we learn of languages, the higher mathematics, and experimental science, although the rudiments of all these are commonly learned before matriculation. This manual is intended chiefly for students who have not the advantages of regular instruction, and very many of these are forced by circumstances to content themselves with the bare necessaries of education. For such the course already marked out is especially designed. It embraces nothing that the commonest education should not include, while it excludes everything else. Having gone thus far in the work of self-culture, the student will now be called upon to decide how much more of regular study he will undertake, and the old questions, " what shall I study?" and "how shall I study it?" will come up again for decision.

In this case, as in the former one, the decision of the question, " What shall I study?" will depend largely upon the student's age, circumstances and purposes. Again he is reminded that in all knowledge there is profit, but that all knowledge is not equally profitable. Again he must remember that there is no limit to profitable education ; that the ideal education is a complete storing of the mind with information, and a complete development of all the faculties ; that the true purpose of education is the preparation of the man for his most perfect work.

Study is the means by which education is secured, and study has a twofold purpose. Whether we study books, men or things, we are constantly accomplishing a double end and receiving a double benefit ; we are acquiring information and we are developing and disciplining our faculties. In deciding between two courses of study, which to select, the student must take into the account the value of the information each will give and the value of the culture each will bring. And these values, as I have before said, vary according to the circumstances and purposes of the student. Some kinds of information and some kinds of culture have a special value in certain businesses, which other culture and other information, equally good in themselves, have not. In other words, the man should be moulded to his work in life as perfectly as possible. The more complete his education can be made the better, but if it must be a partial one, then it should embrace the parts that best supply his wants. I can only indicate the nature of each branch of study, leaving the student to decide which will best serve his purpose, reminding him, however, that he needs them all, and advising him to make the list of his selections as large as his circumstances will allow.

THE SCIENTISTS AND THE CLASSICISTS.

The student who has pushed his education to this point, cannot have failed to discover that there are two opposing schools of educational theorists, differing widely in opinion as to the comparative merits of the two curriculi—the classical and the scientific as they are called. The more conservative school holds that the study of languages brings with it an intellectual culture which nothing else can supply. Their opponents argue that there is nothing, or at any rate very little of practical use, learned from Latin and Greek, and that scientific studies furnish as much mental discipline as the classics do, while their teachings are eminently practical, after the modern acceptation of the term. The classicists accuse the scientists of measuring the value of culture by a sordid utilitarian standard, and the scientists retort by crying " cant," and insisting that the old system of " Latin and Logic " is a musty relic of a less practical age than this.

Between these two it is neither the province nor the purpose of this volume to decide. Probably both are partly right and both partly wrong. The utilitarian character of a scientific education is certainly a point in its favor, but there seems to be quite as much of cant employed in its advocacy as in that of the older system. On the other hand, I am not of those who think lightly of the classics. The culture obtained in study of the languages, whether dead or alive, is of a kind which nothing else can claim to give, while the practical use of such study, even if we confine it to the dead tongues, and measure its value by the strictest of utilitarian rules, is by no means small.

Aside from other considerations, there is no better or surer way of learning English thoroughly than by learning other languages. The kinship of all the Indo-European tongues is so close that we cannot add an acquaintance with any one of them without greatly increasing and improving our knowledge of those we may have learned already ; and in addition to this there can be no question of the fact that the act of translating from any one tongue into any other, is the very best possible exercise for developing that fluency, and freedom, and flexibility in the use of our own language which we all admit are of so much value.

In the exercises given in a former chapter, for the student's use, I have purposely omitted this one of translation, because it seemed out of place there, inasmuch as a large majority of those for whose benefit that chapter was written know no language but their own, and many of them, perhaps, will study no other. Some of those exercises, however, are one in principle with translation, and the processes are, in fact, translations from one kind of English into another. These have been made so for the purpose of supplying to the student of English, as far as possible, the advantages which only the student of other languages can fully enjoy, and the man who would master English, if he cannot study other languages thoroughly, cannot do a better thing than to learn something of other tongues, even if it be but the "little Latin and less Greek" attributed to Shakespeare. The very fact that to learn anything of these he must translate their idiom into our own, is quite enough to justify the recommendation.

I need not dwell upon the advantages of scientific studies. The student will hear these extolled on all hands, and with excellent reason. The sciences deal with the practical concerns of to-day. Their teachings are all of the largest usefulness. Their study equips the student, as nothing else can, for an active, useful, earnest, and profitable life, and anything like a mastery even of any one scientific specialty brings with it a good degree of culture, though the culture is of a somewhat narrow sort in most instances. Indeed, the chief danger incident to scientific pursuits lies in the growing tendency of scientists to follow specialties, to the exclusion of everything else. Humboldt took "all knowledge for his province," but in our day no man can hope to be great in the whole even of any one science. Your botanist, who wishes to be something more than an amateur, confines himself chiefly to some one class of flora. One astronomer studies asteroids, and another makes comets his specialty, until even the fixed stars become, in his view, affairs of minor importance ; while the entomologist thinks meanly of any glass that has a greater range than that of his microscope.

There is so much in science—so much in each separate science—that no one man can grasp it all with a master hand, and as a consequence the tendency is more and more strongly toward specialties. All this, of course, is for the good of science, but it must greatly narrow the men. It is a departure, of the most marked character, from the ideal education—the education which enlarges and develops all the faculties into their fullest and most healthful activity, giving each its full share of culture, and subordinating each to the perfectly balanced whole. It is well for the world that we have specialists, but the pushing of one's whole being into a specialty, while it may ensure good results in that one direction, is not, by any means, the highest or best form of education.

The advantages of mathematical study are manifest. Aside from the practical daily uses of mathematics in every workshop and every office, the study of pure or applied mathematics supplies a kind of intellectual training which can be secured in no other way. The accuracy of conception and statement required, the mastery of principles, the solution of problems—all these develop habits of mind of the most healthful and useful kind. There is hardly any business in which the processes of mathematics are not in constant use, and there can be no position in life in which the mental discipline that comes of mathematical study is valueless.

THE QUESTION TO BE DECIDED.

The student who has completed his common school studies will in almost every case feel called upon to decide what he will select from the seemingly endless list presented by the advocates of the classical and the scientific courses. On the one hand there are a score of separate sciences, almost any one of which is too vast for his complete mastery, and on the other a list of languages still larger. From which shall he select, and how much of either may he safely undertake?

Again, he must decide for himself, having in mind his own special circumstances, the time at his command, his wants in the way of information, and his wants in the way of culture. A careful reading of this chapter will inform him as to the nature of the several branches, and their respective degrees of special adaptation to his purposes, but he should never for a moment lose sight of the fact that the more general and catholic his education can be made, the nearer it will approach to the perfect standard of complete and well balanced culture. If his time is limited, and his business or other circumstances create a special want, let him supply that first, by all means. Otherwise let him beware of the narrowness of specialties. Except in such individual cases as the one named, the best course is one embracing something of the languages, something of the experimental sciences, and something of mathematics—and the more of each the better.*

---

* I speak here only of text-book study. The subject of general literature will be treated under another head.

CHAPTER IV.

HAVING determined to study one or more foreign tongues, the student will almost certainly find himself puzzled to decide what ones they shall be. I cannot tell him, nor can any one else lay down a general rule in such cases. Perhaps I can help the reader, however, to solve the difficulty for himself.

THE COMPARATIVE VALUES OF LANGUAGES.

The Greek and Latin commonly take precedence of modern languages, in systematic curriculi, for the reason that they are much more difficult in some regards, and are therefore supposed to furnish a larger share of mental discipline than any two spoken European languages. Again, our literature, and that of all Europe, is so closely allied to the classics of Greece and Rome as to give special value to the study of those tongues. On the other hand, a knowledge of almost any modern speech is of much greater practical usefulness than a knowledge of Greek or Latin, and the current of opinion seems to be setting strongly in favor of modern languages, in this utilitarian age.

Of the modern languages, French is the most generally useful, perhaps, to people who may have occasion to travel, inasmuch as it is not only the language of diplomacy, but also the one speech in which the traveller can make himself understood almost anywhere in Europe. The French literature, too, is one of the finest in the world.

The German, while it is spoken less commonly out of Germany, is the native tongue of a very large part of Europe. It is so closely akin to the Saxon part of our own language as to have a peculiar value to English-speaking people. And, moreover, there are so many Germans in our own country that a knowledge of their language has a practical value to Americans which no other has.

These are the two modern languages most commonly studied by Americans, for the reason that while their respective literatures are of the very highest order, they have a greater practical value to us than other European tongues. In point of kinship with English the Germanic family of languages (German, Dutch, Scandinavian, etc.) are nearer on one side, and the Latin group (French, Italian, Spanish, Portuguese, etc.) on the other. Most of our shorter, commoner conversational words come to us from the Germanic side, while from the Latin we have the words of nice distinction and more ornate speech. From the one we get the strength and from the other the polish of our tongue. The requirements of the student in one or the other of these regards may influence his choice to some extent, where other considerations are equal.

THE COMPARATIVE DIFFICULTY OF LEARNING THEM.

Another point is the comparative ease or difficulty with which different languages may be learned. To a student who knows nothing but English, the difference in this respect, between the leading languages of the two families, is hardly appreciable. The Dutch closely resembles English in some respects, and the Frisic dialect is so like our own language that travellers have sometimes mistaken it for corrupt English. This is not the case however with the German. We have a good many words in common with that language, but the resemblance is not much stronger than that between English and the Latin tongues, so that the student who knows no language but English will find one about as difficult as the other. With one who knows Latin, however, even partially, the case is very different. To such a person the French and the Italian are much easier than the German, while the Spanish and Portuguese are easier even than these. Indeed, the Spanish is so similar to the Latin that no Latin scholar need trouble himself very much to learn to read it.

If the student knows Latin, then, or any one of the Latin tongues, he will find far less difficulty in learning any other language of that family than in mastering a Germanic speech. If he knows any two of these languages, his study of the others will be still easier.

I suggest all these things merely that the student may have before him all the facts bearing upon the question of what languages he will undertake, and may make his decision wisely.

HOW TO STUDY LANGUAGES.

Languages are studied in a great variety of ways, many of them convenient and many exceedingly awkward. The old system, still in use in too many schools, is to begin with a grammar, study it from beginning to

end, and then, with the aid of a lexicon, to translate
one book after another from the language in hand into
English. The Germans, who have done more than any
other people to develop rational systems of teaching,
were the originators of the first improvements on this
old, slow and unsatisfactory mode of studying languages, and to them we really owe all that we have of
improved methods in the matter. Their first marked
advance was the introduction of what is usually called
prose composition—which consists of a series of graduated exercises in translation—from the foreign into
the mother tongue, and conversely from the native into
the foreign language. The advantages of this plan of
graduated double translations over the old system are
so manifest that the principle involved has found a
place in almost every one of the later methods, most of
which have grown out of it more or less directly.

THE GROUP SYSTEM.

Dr. Beard, in his work on self-culture, predicts that
the discoveries made by the comparative philologists
will revolutionize our system of learning languages.
He thinks the best way to become familiar with different tongues is to study them collectively, and suggests
that the student first take up Sanscrit, as the head of
the Indo-European family, and learn at least those of
its roots which have been preserved in the tongues that
have come after it, and then proceed to learn the comparative grammar of the several languages composing
one of the groups of which the great Indo-European
family is composed.

However admirable this plan may be for men who intend to make comparative philologists of themselves, it

will hardly become, as Dr Beard thinks, the common mode of studying languages, and it certainly has little practical value to the class of students for whom I write. I refer to it here only because it contains the germ of a suggestion which may be of advantage to the student, and that is that if he intends to study more than one language, he will get on faster by studying them in groups, not necessarily beginning with Latin when he means to study that and the tongues which have come from it, but studying all the Latin languages he intends to master, one after the other, deferring those of any other group until after he shall have completed his studies in those of the group first undertaken. In this way one language will become a key to another, and the student's progress will be greatly facilitated.

Ordinarily, however, the number of tongues studied is not sufficient to make this of any practical use, and it will better serve the purposes of this volume to tell the student just how to learn any one language. Several improved plans for doing this have been devised of late years, all of them based upon the German system already referred to, though in them all that system is greatly elaborated and improved.

M. MARCEL'S SYSTEM.

The best of these, in my judgment, is that given in a little book now out of print,* of which I shall endeavor to give the spirit here. In the book itself the reasons for every process and every exercise are given in full, a thing manifestly impossible here, even if it were desira-

---

* The Study of Languages brought back to its True Principles; or the Art of Thinking in a Foreign Language, by C. Marcel, Knt. Leg. Hon., etc., etc.

ble. The student needs only to know what the system is, and that it has proved one of the very best in actual practice. With this general acknowledgment let me give the system of M. Marcel, with one or two unimportant modifications, as briefly as possible.

In learning a language there are four distinct things to be learned. These are—

1. To read the written tongue ;
2. To understand the spoken tongue ;
3. To speak the language ;
4. To write the language.

And these should be learned in the order in which they are here set down, so that one may serve as a key to another. Not that one of these should be, or can be wholly mastered before the next is begun, but this is the order in which they should be taken up. In learning a dead language, the first and last of these are all that it is necessary to know, because the pronunciation of the dead languages is uncertain at best, and as nobody speaks them we have no occasion to learn a questionable pronunciation, which when learned is of no use whatever.

Beyond the quantitive rules of pronunciation therefore there is little to be learned in this respect in the study of dead languages, and the same thing is true also of modern languages, when the student studies them solely with a view to the reading of their literature, and has no purpose to speak or to understand them when spoken.

HOW TO LEARN TO READ A LANGUAGE.

The ordinary way of learning to read a language is by the constant use of the grammar and the dictionary.

In the method now under consideration both of these are dispensed with almost wholly. We not only do not find it necessary to learn the rules of English syntax before learning to read English, but practically we learn those. rules chiefly from our reading, precisely as the grammarians who have written them down for us learned them in the first instance. A language is not made from its syntax, but the syntax is deduced from the language—it is merely a statement of the facts of usage, and is in no way the author of that usage. Accordingly, to learn the rules of syntax which come from the language, before learning the language, is wholly unnatural and irrational. The child learns how to put words together before he learns anything of the syntactical rules involved. He learns to use his mother tongue from the example of others, and not from any rules of syntax, and it is precisely in this way that the student should proceed in learning any other language. He should learn first the usage of the people who write and speak it, and from this he will learn the rules practically without the aid of any grammar.

And the same is true of verbal meanings. Dictionaries only give the translation of words—their equivalents in English—not their meaning in all its fullness, which can only be learned from their use by the people to whom they are natives.

The student cannot learn the grammar of a language or the meaning of its words at all adequately except from the language itself, and to attempt to learn these as a step preparatory to the study of the language is simply an attempt to subvert the order of nature and to accomplish an impossibility.

There are certain things, however, that may be

learned from the grammars and dictionaries as a preparation for reading, and the learning of these constitutes the first step in the study of the language. Let me explain what these are, and briefly state the reasons for learning them and only them. There are two classes of words of which every language is almost wholly composed. The first of these consists of verbs, adjectives and substantives, out of which, chiefly, all sentences are formed. The other class consists of articles, pronouns, prepositions, conjunctions and adverbs, which are used to connect the others or to modify their meaning.

The import of words of the first class varies largely in practice, so that it can only be adequately learned from their use, while words of the other class have ordinarily but a single signification, which may be readily learned ; and moreover, as a rule they have few if any variations of form in composition.

These words of the second class should be so far learned in advance that the student will know them by sight when he shall meet them in reading. There are less than four hundred of them in common use in each European language, and their limited number, together with their usually uninflected character, makes it easy to learn their forms and meanings so that when they are met they will give no trouble.

With words of the first class, however, no attempt should be made to do anything of the kind, but the conjugations and declensions should be mastered, so that the various forms of inflected words may be readily recognized. This much may be learned from any grammar, and this constitutes the whole of the first step in learning to read a language.

The pupil should next begin to translate the foreign tongue into his own language, without the use of dictionary or grammar. When he knows the inflections of the verbs, etc., and can recognize most of the words of the second class, he will have no difficulty in translating any plain text into English, with the help of a strict translation, and for this purpose it is best at first to use text-books in which the English and the foreign text are printed in parallel columns, or on directly opposite pages.

Books of this kind may be had for nearly all the modern languages usually studied in this country; but when they cannot be secured, the next best thing is a translation in a separate volume. Interlinear translations are very perplexing, and are bad for several other reasons.

The books used should be as interesting as possible in their matter, and stories or other works in narrative style are much the best. Poetry should be avoided entirely at this stage of the learner's progress, because it is difficult, and because its syntactical structure is not in accordance with the common usage of the tongue.

The student now proceeds to translate the foreign language into English, referring to his printed translation for assistance, for confirmation in cases of doubt, and for the correction of errors. In the text he has the language in actual use, written by an author to whom it is a mother tongue, and consequently, showing all the usages and idioms of the language much more fully and much more practically than can be done in any ordinary text-book.

What he wants is to learn French, or German, or Spanish just as Frenchmen, Germans or Spaniards

really use it, and this is best learned from a study of it
as they habitually employ it.   He wants no grammatical
disquisition on the subject, and no dictionary translations of words.

He needs to read as much as possible of the lan
guage he is studying, and by thus reading it he finds
out practically what are the usages of the language
and what the real force and meaning of each word is,
and this is just what the grammars and the dictionaries
theoretically teach, but what they can never teach
thoroughly and practically.

But just here it is necessary to remind the student
that translating a book from a foreign language into
English is not reading the foreign language by any
means.   There is much that is untranslatable in every
language.   The full force of an author's meaning can
never be felt except by those who read his work in the
original—that is to say by those who have so far mastered the language in which he writes, that his words
and sentences directly convey his meaning, without
their mental translation into English.

We never know a language, we can never really read
a language, until we can think in it, without mentally
substituting the native for the foreign idiom, or *vice
versa.*

I mention this here, because it should be the constant aim of the student, as he translates, to acquire
the power of understanding the text without translating it.   This power comes only with effort, and the effort should be a constant one, beginning almost as soon
as the student begins to translate.

His first success in this direction will be in the way
of isolated, idiomatic expressions, which cannot be ex-

ac tly translated. Of these he will soon catch the spirit and meaning, at first partially and imperfectly, after awhile in all their fullness. Let him seize every such opportunity, and when once an expression carries its meaning to his mind directly, let him always after avoid the translation of that or similar expressions.

His stock of such will grow much more rapidly than he thinks, and each new acquisition will aid him in se-curing others.

Here is another advantage which this system has over the old one. Grammars and dictionaries teach men to translate only ; by this system we learn to read in the original.

No grammar can tell the student what an idiomatic expression means. It can only tell him what is the English idiom most nearly corresponding with it.

Children learn their own language by precisely this method. No parent lectures his child upon the rela-tions of substantive and verb, before teaching him how to put them together in a sentence. We learn our mother tongue in sentences, and not in words. Even before the child can pronounce at all, he learns to un-derstand what his mother means when she says things to him.

His knowledge of whole sentences precedes his knowledge of words. He can talk and read for many years before he knows anything of syntax, and if he heard nothing but pure, correct English from the first he would use nothing else.

Now it is precisely this system which we should fol-low in learning any foreign language. We should learn not the definitions of isolated words, and the rules of syntax regarding them, but the meaning of the sentences as they are framed by the people whose language we are studying, and thus learn the language itself. After we shall have done this thoroughly, it will be time enough to take up the grammar, if we shall then care to do it.

Let the student begin then by translating some interesting work, substituting actual reading for translation wherever it is possible, and becoming familiar with the usages of the language as rapidly as he can. He will find a second reading of all the passages of very great advantage in this direction, or still better, if he can get for his first reading-book, something with which he is already familiar in English—the New Testament, for instance—he will much more rapidly gain a clear insight into the untranslatable force of the idiom, and acquire much sooner than he otherwise would, the power to think in the language he is learning.

At this stage of the learner's progress, if the language he is studying be a living one, he should make no attempt to pronounce it. The power of understanding the spoken tongue, as will be seen later, must come before that of pronouncing it, and any attempts at pronunciation made before this power of understanding is acquired, will only cultivate and fix bad habits upon the organs of speech employed, and debauch the ear so as to interfere seriously with the ultimate acquisition of a good pronunciation.

At present the student should avoid pronunciation altogether, if possible, letting his eye alone know the words, without attaching to them any idea of sound whatever.

Many people find it impossible to do this, but they may at least avoid the actual pronouncing of the words so that their bad pronunciation may be mental only, and not fix itself upon the organs of speech.

M. Marcel thinks it would be better for the student who must attach some idea of sound to the printed words, to let that idea be precisely what it would be were the same combinations of letters to occur in English, so that when he shall come to learn the pronunciation correctly, he may not be embarrassed by the necessity of correcting approximate but erroneous ideas previously conceived.

The student should continue his translating as rapidly as practicable. What he wants is to become familiar with the words and phrases of the language in actual use, and the more he reads the oftener will each of these present itself.

Repetition is the mother of memory, in the matter of language. The student learns and remembers the exact force of an expression only from its repeated appearance in the text, and the more pages he shall read, the more frequently each word and phrase will occur, and the more he will learn of the language.

At first, of course, he will find a few words whose meaning he cannot discern even by the light of his English translation. For these, and for these only he should consult his dictionary, remembering that it is better always to learn the meaning of a word from its use, when that is possible, than from the verbal translation of a dictionary. For a while it will be necessary to go over every passage two or three times, in order that its full meaning may become clear, and its phrases be fixed in the memory. After a while this will cease to be necessary.

As the student goes on he will rapidly learn the

meanings and the uses of words and of idiomatic expressions. As this knowledge comes to him he must
gradually become independent of his English translation, and learn to rely upon his own increasing knowledge of the language. Beginning with the two texts
in parallel columns, his second or third book should be
wholly in the original, and his translation in a separate
volume, so that he may only refer to it as occasion shall
require.

When he can dispense with the translation except for
very difficult sentences, it will be well to use books with
marginal or foot-notes in which the very difficult passages only are rendered, and to substitute for his
French-English or German-English dictionary, as the
case may be, one written wholly in the language he is
learning, in which definitions in that language take the
place of translations into English.

But it cannot be too strongly impressed upon the student that we learn the true, exact and perfect meanings
of words only by induction after seeing them used in a
variety of ways. We may commit definitions to memory, but we get at the true meaning of words only from
their actual use. This is true to a great extent of our
own language, and still more largely of a foreign one.
When we first meet a word in a sentence we gain an
imperfect idea of its meaning, or we learn one side of
its meaning. When it occurs in other relations we
grasp it more perfectly, and after we have seen it used
a number of times we learn it in all its fullness, and
henceforth know all its purpose and power.

This inductive process is the basis of the system now
under consideration, and to cultivate the habit of induction the learner must work out for himself the

meaning of each word in his text, as far as possible without having recourse to his dictionary.

When the student finds translating without the use of a printed translation thoroughly easy, which is to say, when he shall have learned the use and meaning of most of the words and phrases of the language in hand so that he can readily render the text into its English equivalent, he should set himself earnestly to the work of learning to read in that language without translating it at all, as before explained.

If he has taken care to practice this with single phrases as he has gone on, the purpose will now be much more easily accomplished than it otherwise would have been. He should begin it with the book last translated, because his familarity with the text will greatly facilitate his work. At first he will find it a little difficult, perhaps, to grasp the meaning from the text without the mental act of translation, but a very little practice will enable him to do this, and by constantly reading in this way, he will gradually learn to think in the language, so that he can mentally or in writing frame his thoughts into the forms of the tongue he is learning without first conceiving them in English.

When he can do this readily, he will be able to appreciate the literature of that language, and to read it with a full measure of profit, which he never can do so long as he mentally translates it into his own native idiom.

THE TIME NECESSARY.

With a vast number of students this is all that is wanted of foreign languages. They wish to read and profit by the literature of other nations, and have no especial need or desire to know the spoken tongue. They stop when their purpose is accomplished, and if this be the limit of their purpose, they will naturally want to know how long it will take them to reach it.

To such a question no answer of universal application can be given. The time will vary considerably by reason of differences of mental habit and differing degrees of application and of daily leisure. But a reasonably apt pupil, who can give two or three hours a day to his work, and who works earnestly, should be able to master this much of any modern European language within six months.

M. Marcel thinks that length of time should suffice for this and considerably more, but his estimate is probably based upon his own experience when he gave his whole time and attention to the matter in hand, which few students of course can do.

The dead languages are learned somewhat less rapidly than the spoken ones, but they may be learned, as this much of modern languages may, without any assistance from teachers. Here, as everywhere else, a competent teacher will greatly assist the student, of course, but this much of language the student, with or without a teacher, must really learn for himself, and there is no reason why the want of an instructor should deter any earnest student from undertaking to so far master a language as to read it, to write it, and to think in it.

LEARNING TO UNDERSTAND THE SPOKEN TONGUE.

Every young child hears the conversations around it, . and after a while it begins to understand what is said.

At first every spoken sentence falls on its ear in a confused jumble of sound, which not only means nothing, but is so confused that the child cannot even separate the words from each other, or determine just what sounds are really uttered. Little by little, however, as the same sounds are repeated again and again in its presence, it begins to distinguish them from each other with a constantly increasing accuracy, until it learns at last what certain sets of these sounds mean. *After* this comes its first effort to pronounce the words it has heard.

The order of the process is understanding first, speaking afterwards, and it is precisely in this order that we should put them in learning any foreign tongue. Our organs of speech are exactly like those of Frenchmen, or Germans, or Spaniards, and there is no word in their languages which we may not learn to pronounce quite as well as they. But the difference in the pronunciation of a native and a foreigner in any language, lies chiefly in the niceties of sound, and it arises almost wholly from the fact that the foreign ear has not been educated into the power of distinguishing these niceties of sound in a language other than its own.

At first every foreign language is a confused jumble to our ears, just as all language is to the child, and we must learn to hear it understandingly, just as the child learns to hear his mother tongue. When French is spoken in our presence, if we know no French, it is impossible for us to separate the words from each other, and more than this, we cannot accurately repeat after the speakers the shortest of phrases, giving the sounds as they give them.

To our ears our imitation is exact, but to the Frencn-man it is painfully wide of the mark.   I once knew a French gentleman who said that he lived in this country and spoke English for ten years before he was able to discover the slightest difference in sound between the words "tree" and "three," even when they were utter-ed with the utmost care for the purpose of making the distinction clear to him.   In other words, it took ten years of culture to enable his ear to discover a difference of sound so marked as this.

This much by way of illustration on a point which cannot be too strongly insisted upon, though it is one which both teachers and pupils often overlook,—to wit that the education of the ear should come before that of the tongue,—that we must learn to catch and under-stand the sounds of the language before we can learn to utter them, and that to attempt the latter before attend-ing to the former can only result in bad vocal habits difficult to overcome.

It is for these reasons that we divide this part of the student's work into two separate tasks,—learning to un-derstand the spoken tongue, and learning to speak it.

In ordinary practice the distinction is made loosely when it is made at all, and a great many teachers begin teaching the pronunciation at the outset, even before the student has begun to translate.

To some extent the four parts into which the task of learning a language is divided, overlap each other, of course, and they neither can nor should be wholly sepa-rated, but it is in every way best that the student shall take them up in the order here given, letting them run into each other where they do so naturally, but

treating them, in the main, as separate parts of the work
he has undertaken.

We have already seen that before we can learn to
speak a language properly we must so educate our ear
as to distinguish its sounds nicely, whether they be uttered separately in syllables, or combined into words
and sentences. We must learn to *hear* the language
before we can learn to speak it, and this can be learned
only through the ear.

Books do not address themselves to the ear, and
therefore books can never teach us either to hear or to
speak. For this, and for this only in the study of
language, a teacher is absolutely necessary. The student cannot learn it by himself, and no book can assist
him. He must have a teacher, but any person native to
the tongue, who can read it, will do for a teacher, if he
be instructed a little in the art of teaching what he
knows, and hence I give here some suggestions as to
how the ear and the tongue can best be trained, so that
in the absence of a competent teacher the student may
be able to make use of any person who speaks the language as a mother tongue, himself instructing his teacher how to proceed. A very small expenditure for the
services of some such person will thus cover the whole
cost of learning the language.

It matters little, in this case, whether the teacher understands English or not. All that is required of him
is a correct pronunciation of his own language.

The teacher should begin with a book which the student has recently read, one with which he is thoroughly
familiar. At first he should pronounce slowly and distinctly the words of the book, while the student listens,
with the text before him. A phrase at a time carefully

uttered, and as nearly as possible with the conversational accent, will soon enable the student to follow without
looking at the text, if it be a familiar one, and as soon
as this can be done at all the use of the eye should be
dispensed with, so that the unassisted ear may be
brought into full activity.

When any sound is not accurately caught by the student, or when it does not carry its full meaning with it,
he should stop his teacher and have the words spoken
again and again until their sound and their sense are
perfectly clear.   When exercises of this sort become
easy, the teacher must read whole sentences at once
without dividing them into their clauses, and as soon
as the student can follow him in them he should begin
to increase the rapidity of his reading, taking care that
the increase each day is so slight that the student does
not lose either the sound or the sense of what is
read.

When the student's proficiency is such that he can
readily comprehend a familiar text, read rapidly, one
less familiar should be substituted, and a very few
weeks of diligent application will so train the learner's
ear that he will have no difficulty in understanding any
book read aloud in the language in hand.

It will now be time for him to begin his efforts at
pronunciation.   To make earlier attempts is not only
useless, but positively injurious.   The uneducated ear
imperfectly catches the foreign accent, and the tongue
as imperfectly utters it.   A bad habit of ear is con-
firmed and a bad habit of tongue is created.   But when
the ear clearly catches the sounds of the language, so
that the sound is unmistakable in itself, and carries its
meaning with it, the tongue will be easily trained to the

power of reproducing it, and the well-schooled ear will readily detect and rapidly cure the imperfections of the tongue's performances.

This postponement of the first efforts at pronuncia-tion until after the ear has learned the language, will not only greatly facilitate the learner's progress, but will also make his pronunciation, in the end, much more perfect than it otherwise could be.

As soon as the learner is so far advanced that he can readily understand the reading of his teacher, he should begin the habit of mentally pronouncing after him, as an additional preparation for the task of learn-ing to speak the language, and when he can follow ra-pidly read prose, he should substitute poetry in its stead. As verse is necessarily somewhat involved in style, it cannot be translated quite as rapidly as an or-dinary reader reads it, and hence it is particularly valu-able at this stage of the student's progress, because he must understand it in the original, without translation, if he understands it at all.

The teacher should also talk with his pupil only in the language he is learning, not only for the sake of adding so much to the exercises, but also because in his conversation he will pronounce with the natural ac-cent, a thing which can never be perfectly done in reading.

The student who has learned to read the language easily before beginning this part of his task, should be able to understand the spoken tongue after a month or six weeks of this kind of practice, and he will then be prepared to enter upon the next stage of his journey, namely—

LEARNING TO SPEAK THE LANGUAGE.

In learning to pronounce a foreign tongue the one thing to be guarded against is error. It is far easier and infinitely better to avoid error than to correct it. A word once mispronounced is more difficult to manage afterwards than one that has not been attempted at all.

For this reason it is better not to begin this part of the task at all until the ear is pretty well skilled in its function, after which the pronunciation is readily and correctly mastered. But even when this precaution has been taken, the student should attempt no word until he is sure that he knows its exact sound, to which end the teacher should begin by pronouncing a very short phrase two or three times, slowly and distinctly, the pupil listening until he is sure that he has mastered it with his ear. When this has been done he should take it up in his turn, saying it over until it falls from his tongue without conscious effort.

If he pronounces wrong, the teacher must stop him and repeat the process from the first.

After a little time the length of the phrases may be increased, gradually, until the pupil can repeat whole sentences, slowly at first,—more rapidly afterwards. As the teacher reads, the pupil should attend with his ear only, not looking at the printed page, but taking the words from their articulate rather than their written form. That this may be the more perfectly done, the student should wholly abstain from reading aloud until his pronunciation is fixed. He should learn the spoken language wholly through his ear. He may retain it afterwards by reading aloud, but it cannot be learned satisfactorily in that way.

There are some languages, however, in which the orthography and pronunciation bear a constant and uniform relation to each other—languages in which every letter, and every combination of letters, has its fixed and certain sound. In these, reading aloud as an auxiliary exercise is well enough. In these, too, a very brief tutelage will give the student all the sounds of the language, and enable him by reading to perfect his pronunciation of all the words, without further assistance from a master.

When the student shall have learned to pronounce most of the words in common use, he has only to practice his art, both by reading and by conversation with his teacher, to make himself as nearly perfect in speaking the language as it is practically possible for English-speaking people to become. Should he be surrounded by people to whom the language is a mother tongue, he will of course talk with them only in their native idiom ; but where this is not the case, some care is necessary to prevent the gradual loss of the power to speak in the acquired idiom.

Reading aloud without hearers is not a pleasing task, and hearers sufficiently proficient to follow the reader are not always to be found. To supply this want it is well to commit passages from books to memory, and to repeat them frequently aloud. In other words, the art of pronouncing a foreign language when once acquired can only be retained by practicing it, and anything which furnishes occasion for practice is useful to this end.

I have thus given the spirit of this much of M. Mar-

cel's system, condensing it as far as it is practical to
do so, and altering its details wherever I have thought
a change desirable to adapt it more perfectly to the uses
of that class of students for whom chiefly these
pages are written.   In making these alterations of
detail, however, I have taken care not to depart from
the principle on which his system is based.

I omit wholly the remainder of his teachings,—all
that he says about learning the conversational idiom so
that the pupil's thoughts will flow in it freely, and
all of the chapters on the Art of Writing, on Mental
Culture, and on Routine.   Parts of these have no practical value to students without a master, as they refer
chiefly to the art of teaching rather than to that of
learning.   Other parts are wholly foreign to the purposes of this volume.

As to the art of writing a foreign language, I deem it
unnecessary to say anything, inasmuch as it follows, almost without effort, the art of reading.   Any one who
can read French, for instance, sufficiently well to appreciate the text without translating it, can hardly fail to
write it well, with very little practice.

THE ROBERTSONIAN SYSTEM.

Another very admirable system of learning foreign
languages is that of Professor Robertson.   In its general design it closely resembles the plan already sketched, and in many respects it is but a practical application
of the principles elaborated in M. Marcel's work,
though there are some important points of difference
between the two plans.

The Robertsonian text-books are prepared for use in
schools, and have therefore many things in them, of

which the student without a master cannot make use, but omitting these, the books themselves may be used with advantage by any class of learners.

The text consists of a simple story, so ingeniously constructed that its telling involves all the idioms of the language to be learned, in succession, repeating each constantly, so that even in his earliest lessons the student becomes familiar with all the peculiarities of structure and phraseology, which under the old systems of teaching presented the chief difficulties in his path.

A portion of the text is taken up in each lesson, and printed with a slavish, verbal, English translation interlined. This is followed by a translation into good English. Then follow a series of questions and answers, and sentences for oral translation, made up exclusively of words and phrases from the text, which furnish from the first admirable exercises in double translation, and also rapidly train the pupil in the art of thinking in the language he is learning, and reading it without translating.

This much of each lesson is designed for those who wish to learn the language rapidly and practically. Appended to each of these lessons is a grammatical dissertation for the benefit of those who desire to study the tongue critically as they go on.

The system dispenses, as Marcel's does, with the use of a dictionary, and the text-books are provided with abundant instruction as to the manner of their use, so that the student who shall adopt them will need no guidance of this sort here.

On the whole I prefer the system already sketched to that of Professor Robertson, but the two are so nearly the same in principle that the student cannot err greatly in selecting either, and whether he shall follow the one or the other, his progress will be far more rapid than it could possibly be on the old grammar and dictionary plan.

Before quitting this subject let me give a word of warning to the student—let me remind him that in all education, beyond what is necessary to supply the immediate business wants of the man, culture is of more value than learning ; and with this fact before him the student will readily understand why I say that one language thoroughly mastered is better than a dozen half learned.

If he has taken up French, let him follow that alone, to the exclusion of all other tongues, until he shall have so far mastered its principles as to read it freely and easily. Not until he shall have done this will it be wise for him to begin the study of another language.

CHAPTER V.

THE NATURE AND VALUE OF MATHEMATICAL STUDY.

WE have already had something to say in regard to the value of mathematical study, in the practical usefulness of its teachings and in the culture it brings with it. The practical uses of mathematical knowledge are apparent on every hand, and the culture incident to close, exact study scarcely needs mention.

But there are circumstances which affect the relative value of the mathematics as compared with other studies, and it is necessary that the student who must content himself with a partial education, shall have these in mind in determining how much of the mathematics he will undertake. So far as the bread and butter utility of this or any other kind of study goes,—so far as the question is one of the market value of the learning to be gained, the student will have no difficulty in deciding for himself, as in this respect his decision is dependent almost wholly upon the nature of his proposed business in life. If he is making an engineer or a mechanician of himself, he needs to know all he can learn of mathematical principle and mathematical fact. If he would be a lawyer, or a merchant, or a physician, his practical needs in this matter do not go beyond a good knowledge of arithmetic.

In the matter of culture, however, the case is very different. If the student's business or circumstances are likely to require a habit of close, exact reasoning, careful analysis, and minute investigation, he needs exactly the culture which a study of the mathematics will give him. If his habits of mind are loose and careless, —if he knows himself prone to jump at conclusions, and to accept opinions upon insufficient evidence, if he lacks the power or the habit of discriminating nicely between the probable and the proved, he needs the culture incident to mathematical study, more than discipline of any other sort, and should therefore give the mathematics as large a place as possible in the course he is marking out for himself.

If, on the other hand, his intellectual wants are of a wholly different character, as is often the case, and he has but limited time at his disposal, he may spend that time in something more profitable to him, at least than mathematics.

Again, in some cases, there may be occasion for some drilling in mathematical habits, without the necessity which exists in others for a complete course of the kind.

The question in every case must be decided by the circumstances surrounding that case, and these circumstances the student only can know fully. He should ascertain precisely what his wants are, in the matter of culture as well as in that of learning, and govern himself accordingly.

THE PROCESSES.

The ideal text-book in mathematics is one which explains every principle in the order of its use, and after explaining it, gives the student exercises which enable him to grasp it and to fasten it in his mind. The actual text-book falls considerably short of this, as every teacher knows, and every student finds out.

But in the very nature of things, mathematical text-books are better adapted to their purpose than text-books of any other kind, and there is nothing to prevent any student of ordinary mathematical capacity from proceeding alone from elementary Algebra to the Calculus, with no assistance other than that of his text-books. Indeed, all there is known of mathematics was wrought out originally without even this assistance.

The exactitude of mathematical processes is such that the text-books must of necessity furnish nearly all the aid any earnest student can wish, and hence there is comparatively little for us to say here as to the manner of pursuing studies of this class. A word or two, however, may be of service alike to students in and out of school.

THE ORDER OF STUDIES.

In regard to the order in which the several branches of the mathematics are to be studied, there is very little variation.

We must begin with algebra, of necessity, as it is the basis of all the rest, and while many teachers put their pupils into geometry, as soon as they are fairly grounded in the elements of algebra, it seems to me that the plan is in every way a bad one, giving birth

to much trouble throughout the remainder of the
course, and ending in imperfect scholarship at last.
Such a course is especially bad when the student has
no master, and I have rarely known a case in which
the attempt, on the part of a self-taught student, has
not resulted either in a complete breaking down and
an abandonment of the mathematics altogether, or in a
system of empirical study requiring all the work and
giving none of the culture incident to a complete mastery of the science.

The better plan is to take up first a book on elementary algebra, and to master it absolutely. This should
be followed by Davies' Bourdon, and when the student
shall have completed that, his road through all the remainder of the mathematics will be both an open and
an easy one.

With Geometry, Plane and Spherical Trigonometry,
Analytical Geometry, Navigation and Surveying, which
are the branches commonly studied before the Differen-
tial and Integral Calculus is taken up, the order in which
I have placed them here is as good as any other.

None of them will present any formidable difficulty
to the student who has begun by making his knowledge
of algebra complete, and where this has been done, the
studies enumerated above should not, in the aggregate,
demand more time or more work than was necessary to
the mastery of algebra.

In other words, algebra, if learned thoroughly, is in
time and labor about half the ordinary collegiate course
of pure mathematics. *

---

* Surveying and Navigation are, properly, *applied* and not pure mathematics, but for the sake of convenience I follow here the common classification.

THE WAY TO STUDY ALGEBRA.

When you begin the study of algebra, remember that it is *fact* from beginning to end ; that it has been discovered, and not invented ; that every operation is the application of one or more principles, and that a knowledge of the operations is worth nearly nothing when the principles governing them are not fully understood. What has been said on this point with regard to the study of arithmetic, is, if possible, even more strongly applicable to that of algebra.

Beginning with a clear comprehension of these points, the student should, as far as possible, follow the original process by which the principles of algebra were evolved from each other. He should begin with a full understanding that the science of abstract numbers is a complete structure, made of many parts, each of which was learned in the beginning from those which precede it, and as far as possible he should build the structure piece by piece for himself. To a great extent this may be done without a close following of the book, and where this is the case the text-book should be used only as a general guide, and as a mentor for the verification of work and the correction of error.

Where it is necessary to follow the book strictly, the student should endeavor not only to comprehend each principle, but to discover also just how it follows from those that have preceded it, and how others are to grow out of it.

Almost every new principle will be found to rest upon two or three previously learned, each being a corollary not ordinarily from any single principle, but from a combination of several, and this synthetical process. while it serves to make the student's progress in mathematical study much more rapid and greatly more satisfactory than it otherwise would be, is in itself the very best intellectual exercise incident to this branch of study. Without it one may learn mathematics, though not quite so thoroughly as with it, but in omitting it he loses the greater and better part of the mental discipline and culture to be derived from mathematical studies.

Moreover this habit serves still another purpose in making a study fascinating which is otherwise proverbially dry and uninteresting to the majority of students. Once formed, the habit should be continued throughout the course, but I dwell upon it here because algebra is the basis of all the other branches of higher mathematics, furnishing the groundwork of them all, and whatever is to be done in this regard must be begun at the bottom.

A WAY OUT OF DIFFICULTIES.

As a rule a principle should be thoroughly understood before it is used at all in the working of problems, but sometimes this is impossible, and when the student shall find it so, it will be well for him to proceed with the problems, applying the principle, as yet but imperfectly understood, as a means of grasping it. Sometimes the working of a problem or two will make a matter transparent which before was wholly incomprehensible. But in any event, never leave a principle until you do understand it. Never go on to others until you know what this one is, and the reason for its being

ANOTHER WAY OUT OF DIFFICULTIES.

When the explanations given in the book, and the working of the problems, fail to make the principle stated as clear as it should be to the student's mind, he should at once resort to the simplest available form of using the principle, and the result will almost always be entirely satisfactory.

Let me illustrate my meaning. I had a pupil once who came to a proposition something like this in her algebra :

$$4xab - (2xa + b) = \text{etc.}$$

"By the terms of this equation," the book went on to say, "we have

$$4xab - 2xa - b = " \text{ etc.}$$

The pupil could not understand why, in taking the $2xa + b$ out of parenthesis, the plus signs should be changed to minus ones. She knew very well that there was a rule to that effect in the book, but she was trying to learn algebra rather than the rules of algebra, and so she sought an explanation. She had already worked out three or four problems involving this process of removing terms from parenthesis, but had been wholly unable to grasp the reasons for the change of signs made.

I substituted figures for the letters and wrote the following, as different forms of one equation.

$$20 - (6 + 4) = 10.$$
$$20 - 6 - 4 = 10.$$
$$20 - 10 = 10.$$

Giving her this, I left her to work out the principle involved for herself, and she soon discovered that the 6 and the 4, both positive quantities, were *together* to be subtracted, in obedience to the minus sign, from 20, and the reason for the change of signs in removing the figures from the parenthesis was apparent at once.

I strongly commend such a resort to the simplest form of arithmetical or algebraic expression which can be made to involve the principle, as the very best way of grasping what cannot be comprehended at first in more abstract or complicated shape.

The student will have no difficulty in forming for himself abundant exercises of this kind, adapted to his particular wants as they shall occur.

RULES.

In algebra, as in arithmetic, the rules are merely generalizations after the fact. As such they are very valuable, but the student is constantly in danger of losing sight of their real character, and treating them as rules for the solution of problems.

He should solve his problems on principle, and take the rules as succinct statements of what he has done,—not as rules for what he has to do. He should remember that these rules can have been made only by persons who were already familiar with the processes of which they tell,—that the processes create the rule, not the rule the processes. The temptation to err here is so great that good teachers often regret the presence of any rules at all in the books.

Not that these concise generalizations are valueless by any means. Every teacher knows that they may be made of very great use to the student, if only the principles involved be thoroughly understood before the formulas for their application are learned.

To the schoolboy the danger is far less than to the student without a master, anxious to get on. The former is made to explain his blackboard operations, and thus compelled, to some extent at least, to understand the principles as he applies them. The self-taught youth, on the other hand, has no check upon himself but his own will, and is therefore in constant danger of making a misuse of the rules in his book.

THE OTHER MATHEMATICS.

We have already seen that algebra, thoroughly learned, is not only about half the mathematical battle, but is in itself a key to everything that follows. Geometry, trigonometry, etc., present few difficulties to the student who has mastered his algebra before taking them up for study.

The directions given for the study of algebra are, in the main, applicable to the entire course, and there is little else to be said with reference to the succeeding parts of the mathematical curriculum. With a hint or two we will pass to other things.

Concrete study is always better than abstract, and self-made problems are usually better for practice than those given in the books.

From first to last, therefore, the student should seize every possible opportunity to make problems for himself out of his surroundings, and whenever he can put any principle to a practical test in actual affairs, he will find it a very excellent thing to do.

When he shall have learned enough of mathematics to do so, he will find it a good plan to measure distances by triangulation, beginning with distances which he can verify with his tape line, and passing on to the width of rivers or ponds, and similar practical problems.

Where he studies surveying, he should at once join an engineering party, if possible, doing, in time, all parts of the field and chart work, and observing the work of others. When this is impracticable he should at least spend some weeks in amateur surveying, using his compass or his transit instrument himself, and making his own field notes. When he shall have done this, his notes will furnish him abundant material for chart making, and if he has been at all skillful in the selection of his ground he will have at his hand problems involving nearly all the principles his books have taught him.

Mining and other engineering work, practical mechanics, etc., are within the reach of almost every student of applied mathematics, and the student who would perfect himself should neglect no opportunity of studying them thus practically.

I must add one other suggestion before quitting the subject of mathematics, and that is that the student, especially if he have no master, should be himself a teacher of others if possible. While yet studying algebra he should teach some one else the parts over which he has passed, and so on throughout the course. Teaching others is an excellent aid to the learning of anything, and I once knew a young man who learned Latin entirely by teaching it to a younger brother. He knew the earlier parts of the grammar, and began, half in sport, to teach his pupil. The brother learned rapidly and forced the teacher to learn in order that he might teach, and the end was success for both.

But teaching is especially valuable to the student of

mathematics, inasmuch as it requires constant analysis and a constant explanation of the principles already mastered, and is, withal, the best possible system of review, where reviewing is most necessary. If a student can secure a pupil less advanced than himself, therefore, let him do so by all means, and let him not count the time spent in teaching as lost, or unprofitably used.

CHAPTER VI.

PHYSICAL SCIENCE.

WE have already seen that there are two schools of thinkers in the matter of education, the one advocating the study of ancient languages as the chief part of higher education, while the other estimates such study but lightly in comparison with the learning of physics.

Each of these schools is right, doubtless, or nearly so, in the estimate it places upon its own favorite branch of learning, but each is equally wrong, perhaps, in its valuation of the other. The ideal education embraces both the classics and the sciences, and every education that can claim to be anything like a worthy one must embrace something, at least, of each.

I have already hinted at the practical importance of scientific study, and I have endeavored to suggest some of the dangers incident to a too exclusive pursuit of learning of this kind. I think the inherent and necessary tendency of the sciences to narrow specialties is full of danger to the student, particularly if his mind is not already balanced by a liberal culture in other directions. Of course the great work of scientific research can only be carried forward adequately by scientific specialists, and we must have such men of necessity. But no one of them advances science much.

No one of them grasps enough to do much by himself. No one of them is a scientist in the full sense of the term. Each does his little part, all the more thoroughly because it is so small, and the aggregate result is a grand one. But these little delvers after single facts, who must confine their operations to very narrow limits, and hedge themselves in on every side lest they divide to wasting, do not furnish us models of liberally educated men by any means. *

The story is told of an old German linguist who had devoted his whole life to the study of the Greek article, to the exclusion of everything else, that when dying he cautioned his son against the danger of wasting his energies by attempting too much. " This has been my own error in life," he said. " I have taken the whole article for a study, and it is too great for any one man's mastery. I ought to have confined myself to the dative case."

The aggregate of such men's work is a grand one, and the work is one which could never be done except by men willing to work within these limits.

The world cannot spare men of this kind. Neither can we spare the toilers in mines, but the value of their work does not in any way lessen the peril it brings to the workers.

Let me not be misunderstood. The scientific special-

---

* Of course I am not **now** speaking of the eminent scientific men, who, while they are unquestionably students of specialties, are also broadly cultivated in things other than science, and in science know vastly more than their chosen specialties embrace. Men of this kind are models for all of us, and as will be seen elsewhere, I hold that to be the best practical education which makes its possessor complete master of some one thing, and reasonably familiar with other branches of human knowledge. What the student is especially urged to do is to lay the broadest foundation of general culture possible, and then to do what he wishes to do in any particular direction.

ist does his full share of the world's work and should receive his full share of its honors. He does his work all the better because he works at but one thing. So does the man in a watch factory, who knows nothing about the manufacture of a watch except how to cut the cogs on a single wheel. Neither he nor any one of his hundred fellows could possibly make a watch, but together they produce much better watches than any one man can possibly make.

I say nothing against the system of specialties as a means of forwarding scientific investigation. I only say that the too exclusive study of specialties is not the best form of education for the development of well-balanced men, and that, in this view of the matter, the tendency of all scientific study to run into excess in this direction is a danger incident to it.

I need not detail the advantages of scientific knowledge. They are everywhere evident, and the tendency of the age is to exalt physics, even to the depreciation of everything else.

WHAT PHYSICS TO STUDY.

The student who can push his education beyond the narrowest possible limits, will almost certainly wish to learn something of physical science. That he should do so there can be no doubt. But there are so many branches of scientific study that unless he has some special inducement to some one of them it will puzzle him to determine just what and how much to take up.

There are several points to be considered in deciding the question.

In the first place the sciences are not like the languages. All our tongues are akin, it is true, but they are so far separate and individual wholes that they must ordinarily be treated as almost wholly distinct, when we ask ourselves which of them we will learn. It is not so with the sciences. These so far run into each other as to be in some sense one. They are but parts of a whole—the whole being nature in all her conditions. They are classified separately, but each involves something of the others. Chemistry and natural philosophy underlie most of them, and it is impossible to know any one of them thoroughly without knowing something of at least some of the others.

THE OBJECT SOUGHT.

Now, with this fact in mind, the student must ask himself what his purpose is, in the study of science, and how much time he ought to give to its pursuit. If his object be to advance himself in any business in which a knowledge of chemistry, or of botany, or of mineralogy, or of some other branch of physics will be of special use, let him by all means pursue the study needed.

If he simply wishes to become liberally educated, he will want to know all the more commonly studied sciences at least moderately well.

The subjects with which the several sciences deal are manifest enough to need no explanation, and the student can make his selections advisedly from the first.

HOW TO STUDY PHYSICS.

Science is so largely experimental, as yet, that there can be no such thing as perfect and exact text-books on the subject. The chemists thought for many years after chemistry became a recognized branch of physical study, that water was an elementary substance, and when the idea that it is a compound was first put forth, it was stoutly denied by nearly all the chemists of the day. Now our greatest scientists do not feel at all certain that they have as yet discovered any absolutely elementary substance. They are more confident of carbon in this respect than of anything else, but they readily admit that even carbon may prove to be a compound. Everything about what we ordinarily call the sciences is in a state of development and progress. We are learning new facts and correcting old errors every day. Every branch of scientific study is changing its teachings, and therefore there can be nothing like permanency in the text-books, and none but the latest of these should be used.

This is the first point to be observed. Let the student get the very latest recognized authorities in every case, and when he shall come to study them, let him remember constantly that their statements of fact are in many cases only statements of the best received opinion as to facts still under investigation, and still but uncertainly known. It is only in this spirit, and with this understanding, that he can hope to benefit himself largely by the study of physics.

The facts just stated lead, too, to another injunction. The student who would make himself anything more than a mere parrot in his knowledge of physical science, must be to some extent a pioneer. He may accept authority in a general way, but he should always feel himself free to reverently doubt its conclusions, and to test them for himself by personal observation and experiment. There is no other way of accomplishing any worthy results in these branches of human learning, and I put these cautions at the fore, for the reason that their absence results in so many failures.

In the study of science, whether on a large or small scale, whether in a general or a special way, no instructor is at all necessary to the earnest student. The rudimentary parts are all easily learned from the text-books, and in our day there is no lack of able and exhaustive treatises of a higher sort. All these may be mastered quite as well without as with a teacher, and while the apparatus and the collections of specimens in our colleges furnish excellent aids to the study of all the sciences, their absence is not fatal by any means. Plates supply their places in part, and a little industry will enable the student to supply them still further in many ways.

I know a woman, living in a retired country place, who without teachers has made herself an accomplished botanist, and not only so, but she has, little by little, accumulated an herbarium that would do honor to a college, and her country garden has a botanical corner where she has tested rare plants from every quarter of the world.

I know a young man, too—or rather a boy, for he is hardly of age yet—who, with very meagre educational advantages of any sort, has so far mastered natural history as to have attracted the attention of distinguished professors, who have been glad to avail themselves of his services as an assistant in their work. His collection of specimens, too, is a very creditable one.

I mention these things for the encouragement of students who wish to follow scientific studies, but doubt their ability to accomplish the purpose worthily without instructors and without access to the collections and cabinets of the colleges.

So far as the sciences can be learned from books at all, they may be learned without masters. Beyond this the student will ordinarily have no need to go, unless he wishes to make a specialist of himself, and in that event he must resort to direct investigation on his own account, attaching himself, if possible to scientific expeditions, or in some other way securing the best conditions of study at his command.

CHAPTER VII.

MORAL AND INTELLECTUAL SCIENCE.

THE VALUE OF THIS KIND OF STUDY.

In marking out his schedule of studies there is no class of subjects which the self-guided student so often overlooks as that which forms the subject of this chapter.

It is worthy of remark that in the University of Virginia, and other institutions where the studies are optional, and where men graduate separately in the several schools, the students who do not work for degrees more frequently omit studies of this class than those of any other. I have even known students in these institutions, who graduated in all the schools but this, and left without degrees, because they deemed the study of intellectual science so wholly valueless that they could not afford to devote to it even the limited time which would have been necessary to add its diploma to their others, and thus to secure their degree.

THE CAUSE OF THE MISTAKE.

The mistake is a very natural one, doubtless, but none the less serious on that account.

In our age and country the utilitarian idea has become so strong that it often transcends its proper limits.   People who measure everything by its practical value, are very apt to see utility only in those things which bring money to the purse ; and further than this they nearly always fail to reach sound conclusions even in this respect, by falling into the error of looking only at the value of the *learning* acquired in particular studies, estimating the culture at nothing.

A moment's reflection should show the student the fallacy of both of these conclusions.   Inasmuch as money is by no means the only good to be sought in life, things which do not add to the ability to make money may be quite as useful and quite as practical as those that do ; and in estimating even the money value of education, the culture it brings is quite as worthy of consideration as the learning incident to it.

THE VALUE OF THESE STUDIES AS A MEANS OF CULTURE.

Now as a means of high culture there is hardly any part of the college course more valuable than the studies embraced under the general head of moral and intellectual philosophy.   It is true too that these studies are peculiarly valuable, even if they be measured by the most strictly practical standard.

The object of education, as we have already seen, is to fit the man for life ; to prepare him to fill, as perfectly as possible, his place in the world ; to enable him to do his best work for himself and for others, and certainly no one should doubt that the cultivation and development of the reasoning faculties, and their instruction in the laws which should govern all their operations, are matters of moment to this end.   At every step in life we are called upon to use precisely the faculties which are cultivated by studies of this class, and at least half the failures and nearly all the blunders we make result from the imperfect or perverse action of these faculties.

Of course no amount of training can make our judgments perfect, or enable us to reason infallibly on any speculative subject ; but from the study of intellectual philosophy we learn the principles of sound reasoning and cultivate habits of correct thought, which cannot fail to serve us in good stead throughout life.

Reason is our crown of glory. It is the ability to reason that chiefly distinguishes us from brute beasts, and elevates us above them, and certainly there can be no part of education more to be desired than that which deals with this faculty, teaches us its nature, and its laws, and trains us in its use.

THEIR VALUE AS A PREPARATION FOR OTHER STUDY.

But aside from all this, the studies of this class are peculiarly valuable as aids to the mastery of others. The student who has trained himself somewhat in the ability to reason logically, and has cultivated that ability by following out the ratiocinations of able thinkers in the text-books which follow Logic, will find far less difficulty in his study of mathematics and the physical sciences than he otherwise would, while the still larger education which comes from within rather than from without—the education of intelligent and systematic thought, can only come fully to those who have, in one way or another, cultivated themselves in this direction.

Of course I do not mean to say that the art of reasoning correctly is wholly an art to be learned, or that there are no studies other than those we are now considering, which serve to cultivate and develop the facul-

tics in question. The mathematics do this in a very
large degree, and other studies help, too, in their several
ways. Even outside of study altogether, men cultivate
the reasoning faculties constantly. But faculties so all-
important as these should receive the best possible
training and the fullest measure of it. It is not enough
that we shall reason approximately well ; we need to reason at our very best, and to this end we need not only to
exercise and cultivate these faculties of mind, but also to
inform them fully as to their own processes, the rules that
should govern them, the errors into which they are apt
to fall, and the tests by which the accuracy of their
operations can be measured. To this end we need to
learn logic theoretically and to familiarize ourselves with
its applications in the text-books which follow logic in
the regular order of studies.

In addition to all this, we find in the course of study
now under consideration much practical wisdom that
every man needs ; inasmuch as our moral perceptions
are never so keen or so perfect as they should be, we
cannot fail to derive great benefit from a study of systematic ethics. While we are yet children we may
govern ourselves in the matter morals by the precepts
of our natural advisers and guardians, but when we
become men and women we need such a grounding in
the laws of morality that we shall be able to govern
ourselves intelligently without leading-strings. Education contemplates the development and culture of the
whole man,—the ripening of all his faculties, mental,
moral, and physical, and the education which does not

include the culture of the moral sense and its subjection to law, is lamentably deficient.

The. other studies of this class are similarly valuable. Our knowledge of English can never be what it should be. until we shall have learned something of the laws of figurative language, which, though not strictly a part of intellectual philosophy, are so nearly akin to it as to be classed with it in most courses of study. There is nothing in which young writers and speakers are more apt to blunder than in the use of figures of speech, and it is no uncommon thing for a reader to lose the force of a passage or to misconceive its meaning totally, from a want of just this training.

The same thing is true of the other parts of Rhetoric. They serve to perfect the student in the use of his mother tongue, and should if possible be added to the course of English study already prescribed in a former chapter.

Political Economy deserves a large share of the attention in any case, and with us, in a country where the people govern, or more properly, perhaps, where they could govern if they would, there is certainly no subject of speculative study so universally needed.

We all complain of mob rule, of the tyranny of parties, of the reign of rings and cabals and cliques ; we all lament the corruption and the venality of our politics, and yet we have only ourselves to blame for the lamentable facts of which we complain. We take no trouble to inform ourselves upon the principles of government. We attach ourselves to parties. We call ourselves Democrats or Republicans as our prejudices may dictate, and blindly vote for the men nominated by the selfish managers of these parties, taking their doc-

trines of governmental policy and their personal **hon-
esty** upon trust, until our elections have come **to be**
little more than a scramble for spoils.

Now and then we meet men who dare to be independent of party, and vote intelligently for the weal of the
state ; but these are few indeed, and the great majority
even of otherwise intelligent men vote the ticket
of their party without inquiry as to the correctness of
its principles, the wisdom or justice of its policy, or even
the personal rectitude and trustworthiness of the men
it commends to their suffrages.

Every political platform is simply an insult to all intelligent men.　These documents profess to set forth
the doctrines and policy advocated by the party and
represented in its candidates.　In point of fact they do
nothing of the kind.　They are simply cleverly executed
palimpsests which may be read either way ; they are ingeniously contrived traps for the catching of votes, and
when once their purpose has been served, nobody ever
thinks of holding the officers, who have been elected
upon them, to an honest fulfillment of their promises.

These are notorious facts, and in them lies, without
doubt, the greatest danger to which our republican institutions are exposed.　We are, as a people, altogether
too ignorant of political economy, and we care too
little about it.

If we would govern ourselves well, and free ourselves from the despotism of corrupt parties, we must
take the matter really and truly into our own hands.
We must inform ourselves upon the laws of political
economy and be prepared to vote as our convictions of
justice and policy may dictate, without regard to the
consistency which demands a perpetual adherence to a

party name; and when any considerable portion of the American people shall do this, even though it be but a respectable minority, its possession of the "balance of power" will compel a purification of parties, and force them to set forth clearly, distinctly and honestly their real principles and purposes, and to carry them out faithfully when in power.

That such an end is greatly to be desired, nobody will deny, and it can only be accomplished by individual efforts. But if it shall never be reached even approximately there is still no reason why the student should neglect to make himself as intelligently capable as possible, of the performance of his duties as a citizen.

THE ORDER AND METHODS OF STUDY.

Having glanced thus briefly at the value and importance of studies of this class, we come now to the question of the order and the methods of their pursuit.

Except that Logic underlies most of them to a great extent, and should therefore be the first of these subjects taken up, there is no very necessary order of sequence to be preserved, and should circumstances make it desirable to alter the order I shall give, there will be no harm done. Otherwise I think the student's progress will be more systematic and satisfactory if he will take them up somewhat as they are arranged below.

He should begin with Logic, and his text-book need not be a very large or a very costly one. A compact, concise treatise on the subject will give him its principles fully, and enlighten him sufficiently in regard to the modes of their application. A very excellent manual of this kind was issued some years ago by Profes-

sor Coppée, of the United States Military Academy at
West Point. The first edition, which is the only one
I have seen, was full of typographical errors, many
of them marring the sense ; but this defect has doubtless been cured in later editions. If so, I know of no
better work on the subject for the use of students without masters. Its statements of principle are singularly
clear and concise ; its illustrations are very apt, and its
brevity and cheapness are greatly in its favor.

With such a text-book, of which there are several of
nearly equal value, the student can easily master the
elements of Logic. He will need only to read it carefully twice—the first time slowly, that he may understand its principles in detail, the second time more rapidly, that he may fix the system, as a whole, in his
mind.

He should then take up Rhetoric, studying it very
much in the same way, but adding to the study of the
book such exercises as will readily suggest themselves
for the fixing of its rules in his mind, and for intelligent practice in its teachings.

Archbishop Whateley's and Professor Coppée's treatises are as good, perhaps, as any others as elementary
text-books and their study should be followed by the
perusal of works of a more elaborate kind on the subject, such, for instance, as Campbell's Philosophy of
Rhetoric.

After completing the study of elementary Rhetoric,
however, and before reading more exhaustive works on
the subject, the student should read Lord's Laws of
Figurative Language, or some similar manual, as a proper supplement to the study of systematic Rhetoric in
its elementary form.

Next in order should come Ethics, and for an elementary text-book, I know of nothing better than Dr. Francis Wayland's Elements of Moral Science, which is used more generally, perhaps, than any other, in the colleges of this country. It needs only a careful reading, to make its principles clear to the student's mind, and it should, if possible, be followed by some more elaborate work on the philosophy of morals, such for instance as Coleridge's Aids to Reflection, or Victor Cousin's The Good, Beautiful and True.

Many students will find in the list already given as much labor as they can well devote to abstract studies of this kind. They will already have learned something of metaphysics, and will have no time to devote to the study of intellectual philosophy, pure and simple. These will need to pass at once to Political Economy.

But where the limitations of time are not so narrow, I strongly recommend a course in mental philosophy, strictly so called, and it should properly follow the studies we have just considered.

The student should read Lord Bacon's Novum Organum, Locke on the Understanding, and Brown's Philosophy of the Human Mind, as text-books, to which, if he wishes to extend his philosophical reading, he may add, with advantage, the works of Herbert Spencer, Sir William Hamilton, Dr. McCosh, President Noah Porter, John Stuart Mill, and others, as occasion may serve.

The line between systematic, text-book study, and general reading is here so narrow that I add the foregoing catalogue of books in this place, though most of them belong rather to the chapter on General Read-. ing.

We come next to Political Economy ; and here again it is very difficult to draw the line between study, in the schoolroom sense of the term, and general reading. I content myself, therefore, with remarking that the student needs first to acquaint himself with the principles of political economy from some good text-book—Dr. Wayland's Elements is the best one for the purpose, I think—and then to read as largely on the subject as he can, taking care to examine both sides of the questions on which our political philosophers differ widely. The chief of these is Free Trade vs. Protection, and on such a question the student should at least hear what both the schools have to say. If he has preconceived notions on the subject, as most of us have, there is the greater necessity for an examination of the arguments of the writers with whose conclusions he is at issue. For a brief but pretty complete course of reading on the subject I would recommend

 Adam Smith's " Wealth of Nations ;"
 John Stuart Mill's " Principles of Political Economy;"
 Mill's " System of Political Economy ;"
 Horace Greeley's " Science of Political Economy," and
 H. C. Carey's " Political Economy."
And these may be read in any order of sequence, without material change of result.

I name these for the benefit of students who desire merely to make themselves familiar with the general features of the subject. Those who wish to study it thoroughly as a specialty, will of course read Bentham, De Quincey, Malthus, Colton, M'Culloch, and a score of other authors.

A similar enlargement of the course in other directions—logical, ethical or otherwise—will suggest itself to students who wish to make any of these a subject of special study, and for information as to the various books extant of these and other kinds, reference may be had to The Best Reading, a book published by Messrs. G.P. Putnam & Sons, in which the principal works on every subject are given in the alphabetical order of their authors' names, under alphabetically arranged titles as to subject, class, etc., and their comparative standing in literature indicated as nearly as practicable. The book may be had for a trifle, and cannot fail to be of very great service to any person who intends to read at all extensively, or to collect even the smallest library.

Even where no such purpose exists, such classified dictionaries of books are valuable as reading matter, as will be seen in our next chapter.

CHAPTER VIII.

GENERAL READING.

SOME WORDS OF WARNING.

THE student who shall follow at all adequately the course of study sketched in the preceding chapters, will, at its conclusion, have completed a very fair curriculum, and he will be master of most of the branches included in an ordinary collegiate education.

But by all means let him not make the mistake, too often fatal even to collegians, of supposing that his education is in any sense complete, and that he has enough either of the information or of the culture which constitute an education. In point of fact he has only learned how to educate himself and mastered the rudiments of his life studies. He has yet to read extensively, and to think,—to study general literature and to study men and things; he has yet to become complete master of himself,—to learn much in the school of self-criticism, to apply what he has learned to the practical affairs of life, and to make it his guide to the acquisition of larger measures of information and culture,—he has all this to do if he would reap the full rewards of his labor. And should he continue his work for a lifetime, there will still be more unlearned than learned, and the culture will still be imperfect.

The point I would here enforce is simply this, that the course of study marked out for the student here and in the colleges, constitutes nothing more than an introduction to the real work of securing ripe scholarship and thorough culture.

I would have the student learn that there is more of information and infinitely more of culture to be gained in the study of general literature and in actual intellectual work, than in the most thorough of collegiate trainings.

As a preparation for profitable reading and successful work, regular systematic study cannot be too highly esteemed, but it should never for a moment be mistaken for the end to which it is only the means.

If, therefore, the student's time is so limited that his pursuit of systematic study will seriously abridge his after reading and other intellectual work, I strongly urge him to forego the former in large measure for the sake of the latter ; to content himself with a thorough mastery of the common school course I have recommended, and the merest outline of the one following it, that he may have time for the higher and better education of the library.

Extensive general reading may make cultivated, well-informed, well-balanced men without much knowledge of the text-books ; but no amount of text-book study, without extensive reading, ever yet brought about such a result.

I argue now, not *against* systematic study, but *in favor* of general reading. The study of text-books is an admirable beginning in the work of education, but it is

not the whole of that work.   It is a means and not an
end.   It is very valuable, but not absolutely necessary
in all cases, while a general acquaintance with literature,
a large reading of books, is necessary always to anything
like thorough culture, and may, by itself, accomplish the
result.

Now, if the reader be indolent and inclined to self-
indulgence, he will almost certainly construe these remarks into an easy excuse for his neglect of text-
books, and I cannot help it.   He may rest assured, however that indolent people are not the ones who manage
to make reasonably well-educated men of themselves
without much acquaintance with text-books, and that in
any event his readiness to abandon **the** more laborious
preliminary task argues badly for his success in the
after work.

The training of the regular course is the best possible
preparation for the self-culture that comes after it, and
the young man who deliberately omits this preparation
gives small promise of success without it.

The purpose of this volume is to tell the student
what constitutes education, and how to secure as complete a one as his circumstances will permit.   To
this end I must show him the comparative importance of the several parts of his work, so that he may
select judiciously where he must select some parts of
the whole to the exclusion of others.   My advice to
every reader is,—Make your education as thorough, as
wide, as complete and as well balanced as possible, but
if you must omit some things belonging to the regular
scheme, get all the light you can in regard to their comparative values, and then select, for omission, those
which are the least necessary, remembering all the time

that every such omission is a loss which you cannot afford to sustain, if you can possibly help it. And this is precisely the extent of my meaning when I say that, as between text-book study and general reading, the preference should be given to general reading.

AN EXCEPTION.

To all this, however, there is one exception which must be made. In cases where for any good reason the student's purpose is the mastery of a specialty, he must of course make the text-books bearing on that specialty the basis of all his work, and must master them absolutely. But even this is an exception only in appearance, for students of this class, after they shall have mastered the text-books in their particular line, if their time is limited, will do better to pass at once to more general reading on the subject they have in hand, than to devote themselves to the study of text-books foreign to their purpose.

WHAT TO READ.

There is no question more frequently asked than " What shall I read?" Certainly there is no question more difficult to answer.

No man ever yet read all that he might have read with profit, and no reading man ever read half that he would have liked to read. The best that any of us can do in the matter is to do our best. That is to say, we can only read a part of what we need and would like to read; governing our selections in this, as in every thing else, by the circumstances in which we are placed.

An intelligent conception of the object we have in

view, however, and a little attention to the peculiar service which each particular class of literature is capable
of rendering us, will greatly aid us in determining in
a general way what we will read, and for the rest we
must trust largely to accident and impulse.

If a man read only for amusement, he is very apt to
read the most entertaining books within his reach, but
in such cases accident has a large share in determining
his selection. I have even known fairly intelligent men,
when shut up under stress of weather at a country inn,
where they could get nothing else, to read the dreary
drivellings in sentimental annuals, rather than listen to
the drearier drivellings of a tiresome landlord.

In these and similar cases, accident is the evident
determiner of the choice. But even where the stress of
circumstance is not so sore, at least half our reading is
in part accidental, or the result of impulse. And, after
all, if the taste be reasonably well cultivated, and there is
no special end in view, it is a pretty good plan to follow
the advice of an old reader, who, when requested by a
youngster to mark out a *liberal* course of reading for
him, wrote in reply, "Read just what you wish to read,—
that is the most liberal course I can suggest."

Even this, however, is a course of reading impossible
to follow fully, for who that reads at all ever succeeded
in reading half that he wished ?

But the taste is not always well cultivated, and so is
often an unsafe guide.

Again, men do not all read merely for amusement, and
those who care to make use of this manual are only
those whose reading is for a definite purpose of some
sort, general or particular. Now the differences of purpose on the part of different people make all the differ-

ence in the world in the answers that should be given to the question we are considering.

The first thing to be determined, therefore, is the purpose for which you intend to read, and the purposes of different people in this regard are as various as can well be imagined.

I remember hearing a young man ask an old reader what he should read, when a conversation something like this ensued:

Old Reader.—What do you want to read for ?

Young Man.—That is rather a difficult question to answer.

Old Reader.—Very well. But you must answer it before I can possibly advise you what to read. If you wish to become a physician, I would strongly advise you to read standard medical works in preference to any others. If you aspire to the law, you might begin with Blackstone as an introductory work, following it up Kent's Commentaries and——

Young Man.—I don't want anything of that sort ; I only want to inform myself generally.

Old Reader.—Very well. But I doubt that. Do you mean that you really wish to become a well-informed man, or do you merely wish to appear so—to be able to join in conversations on a great variety of subjects, and make a fair showing in society ?

The young man admitted that this last was about his idea, though he seemed to have just discovered the fact.

"Very well, I say again," said the old reader, "your object is a very common one, and is easily accomplished. You have only to read Burton's Anatomy of Melancholy. If you can stand a little more, it would be well enough to add Shakspeare to the list. The Bible you will read, of course."

The old reader was right. The purpose the young man had in view is a very common one, and the shortest possible road to its accomplishment is the one his adviser pointed out.

The incident serves also to show how essential it is to an intelligent selection of reading-matter that the prospective reader shall know precisely what are his objects in reading. In this, as in everything else, he should ascertain what he wants before he sets about the task of selecting it.

And yet this is rarely done. People who want to read are very apt either to trust blindly to accident, or to ask somebody to mark out a course for them to follow, or to adopt from some autobiography or other the course its author wishes that he had followed.

COURSES OF READING.

As a rule, set courses of reading are not advisable. In the first place, the cases in which they are faithfully followed are very few indeed, and where they are begun and after a while abandoned, a serious injury is done to to the reader, by his failure to carry out a purpose deliberately formed.

But aside from this, it is impossible for any person to decide, in advance of the reading, just what set of books will best accomplish his purpose. Suppose, for the sake of example, that the student wishes to make himself acquainted with the history of the times of the Stuarts. At the outset his course seems plain enough. There are half a dozen histories to be read, and a few books of the period to be looked over. But before he shall have fairly started in his first history he will find that he needs to know something of the history of England previous to the accession of James the First. Then he will find that a clear comprehension of this much of English history is only possible to people who know, in a general way, the history of Europe during the middle ages. He will want also to know the causes of the Reformation, and of the peculiarities of the English revolt from Catholicism. To this end he must read something of church history and theological controversy. Many such necessities will arise, and it is hardly probable that the student can have marked out in the beginning just the books he now finds it necessary to read. He must either abandon the course originally determined upon and adopt a very different one, or else he must go on with the consciousness that he is allowing his preconceived rule of action to thwart the purpose it was designed to further.

All this is still more applicable, of course, to those cases in which the purpose is wider and more comprehensive than the one supposed above. It is not possible that the student, before he has begun his course of reading, can be at all competent to decide of what that course shall consist.

And the case is not changed materially by the calling in of a friend to act as adviser, for the best that he can do practically is to mark out two or three or four courses, between which the student must himself choose, and this is precisely what he is incompetent to do wisely.

The better plan, and indeed the only plan at all practicable, is to determine clearly your purpose in reading, and then to choose your books as you go on, with strict reference to that purpose. You will find at every step abundant suggestions as to the next books to be taken up, and the only embarrassment with which you will meet will be that arising from the very multiplicity of desirable text-books.

I once knew a literary man who wanted to write an article on cats, and knowing very little about the subject he set himself to work reading up. He told me that in the outset he expected to find nothing about the animals in question, outside of the encyclopedias and natural histories. His first examination of one of these suggested four books to be consulted. These made frequent reference to others, and becoming interested in his subject he bought, before he knew it, a whole shelf full of cat literature, and then, as a matter of economy, began to frequent the great public libraries in search of the hundreds of other books from each of which something was to be learned about cats. He quitted the subject at last, but felt in quitting that he had not exhausted it.

Precisely the same thing may be done in any direction, and the only difficulty often is to know when to quit the pursuit of a topic for something else, and here again the predetermined purpose will be the best guide.

SOME GOOD RULES.

Believing as I do that prearranged courses of reading are not advisable, I shall of course mark out none, and holding that the reader should in every case decide for himself what he will read, I shall make no attempt to decide for him. But a few suggestions may enable him to see his own way more clearly.

READING UP.

Of course, when there is a particular subject on which the student wishes to inform himself, his only course is to "read up" on it, as the hack writers say, and the extent to which he should do this will be measured in each case by the extent of the need suggesting it. If he desires to make himself thorough master of a specialty, in all its bearings, he must read carefully everything he can find having reference to it. If he merely wishes to acquaint himself generally with the subject, a less elaborate reading will suffice.

There are many people who do all their reading in this way, and in the end they become pretty well informed on most subjects, but I doubt the wisdom of such a course where there are no circumstances to make it necessary. It is not productive of as much culture as other systems are, and people who practice it are very apt to read nothing at all at times when they have no special subject in hot chase. And yet the plan has the sanction of some great names. Among others Richard Brinsley Sheridan and Oliver Goldsmith are notable examples. It is related of the former that on one occasion, when a great financial question was under consideration in the House of Commons, he announced that he intended to speak upon it. His friends received the announcement with wondering smiles, as Sheridan was proverbial for his utter ignorance of figures. He had four days, however, in which to "read up," and at the end of that time he delivered one of the most masterly arithmetical arguments ever heard in the House.

His success showed what he could do in the way of

"cramming;" but with all his brilliancy, it can hardly be said that Sheridan was a very good model for anybody's following.

READING TO CURE DEFECTS.

There is one respect, however, in which it is very desirable that all our reading should be to some extent of this character. As in text-book study, so also in general reading, an effort should be made to supply defects both of information and of culture. The weak places need, and should have a constant strengthening. It is in these points that we fail, and it is of the utmost importance that our intellectual armor be made as complete and perfect as possible.

To this end the student must carefully study himself as his master would study him, recognizing every fault and every defect, in order that he may know clearly what he has to supply.

So far as the mere acquisition of information is concerned, this task is an easy one, but in the matter of culture it is more difficult, though even here we may know ourselves reasonably well if we choose to make the effort fairly and with as little prejudice as possible. Indeed we must do it, if we would make anything like well-balanced men and women of ourselves.

Having discovered important defects in his culture or his stock of information, the student should give himself at once to the work of curing them by reading such books as are best adapted to the accomplishment of that end.

READING TO STRENGTHEN STRONG POINTS.

On the other hand, if the student recognizes in him

self any point of peculiar strength—anything in which he is likely, from peculiar constitution or taste, to achieve an especial success, it will always be best for him to subordinate everything else to the cultivation of the one faculty which constitutes his strength.

READING BOTH SIDES.

In either case, whether the student reads for the full rounding of his education or for its perfection in a single direction, there is nothing more important than that he shall read both sides of every question he shall take up. If he read Hume's History of England, for instance, that reading will make Lingard almost a necessity to him.

That this is true of all speculative and historical literature is apparent, but the principle has a wider application than this. Even in matters of mere taste it is well to cultivate catholicity, and so it is a good plan to select poetry and other imaginative literature with reference to the cultivation of a wide and generous appreciativeness that shall embrace something more than a single school of poets or novelists. Mr. Thackeray rejoiced in his daughter's persistent and perpetual reading of Dickens, but it would have been greatly better for her had she turned sometimes from Nicholas Nickleby to Vanity Fair, even if she had made no more radical change of intellectual diet, for the prevention of intellectual dyspepsia.

HOW MUCH OF A BOOK TO READ.

Inasmuch as we cannot possibly read half or even a tenth of the books we would like to read, it is very important that we waste no time reading the less desirable portions of the books we do take up.

It is a rule often laid down for readers that they should never begin a book without going entirely through it. Now if every book contained only cream, and if there were only a very few books in the world worth reading, this would be excellent advice. But unfortunately there is a good deal of very thin skim-milk in many books that have some cream in them, and there are many more valuable books than any one can read.

When our purpose with a book has been served— when we have read those parts of it that we want, it is simply a waste of precious time to go on reading the parts that we do not particularly want, even though they be good in themselves, when there are so many other books that we greatly need to read.

Suppose, for instance, that you are studying the subject of popular education. In the middle of Mr. Herbert Spencer's Social Statics there is a chapter bearing upon the subject which you must certainly read. When you shall have read that, it would be simply absurd for you to go on and read the remainder of the book, although every chapter of it is valuable. You are reading for a particular purpose, and you have many books to read before that purpose will be accomplished. The one chapter is all that this book has to offer you in this particular direction, and you certainly cannot afford to spend time that should be given to other works on the subject, in reading the excellent chapters of Social Statics which do not bear upon it.

Dr. Johnson's advice was much sounder. His maxim was, " When you open a book, and become interested in the middle of it, never stop to begin at the beginning." The rule is a very good one in its letter, and a much better one in its spirit, which clearly is that we should take pains to get at what we want in every book, with as little loss of time as possible. Himself an omnivorous reader, he knew thoroughly well the art of getting promptly at the kernels of all his books.

READING ABOUT BOOKS.

To be at all well-informed, one must know a good deal about books which he cannot possibly find time to read. He must know the authorship, the character, and history generally of vastly more books than he could possibly read in half a dozen lifetimes. He must know whence they came, what peculiar circumstances are connected with them, who their authors are, to what discussions they have given rise, what their effect upon the world has been, and what is their literary level. Not that all these things can be remembered in every case, or that they should be even deliberately studied in detail. But one's reading should at least have some reference to this, and he should seek to become thus acquainted with literature as a whole.

To this end even publishers' catalogues are not without value, particularly when they are at all full in their descriptions. But much better than these are well digested books about books, such as the one already referred to.* Such a volume may be had for a trifle, and in addition to its value for reference, it has the additional merit of furnishing its reader a comprehensive view of literature as it is, and a well digested index to the subject he has in hand. The reader who shall give a day or two to such a volume will learn what every person must know more or less thoroughly to be

---

* The Best Reading.

well informed—namely, what books each author has given to the world ; who is the author of each of the books we hear spoken of in conversation ; to what class of literature each belongs ; of what it treats, and what is the position assigned to it in literature by the best of our critics.

He will learn, in short, the outside of literature,—he will have before him an excellent map of the literary world, and will gain from it a valuable knowledge of those parts of it over which he cannot travel in person.

But it is not enough that he shall know this much of the books which he cannot hope to read. There are very many of the books that we have no time to read, about which we need to know something more than their titles and similar matters, and this is most readily accomplished by the reading of intelligent criticism.

Of some books an elaborate review is worth reading, but these, for the most part, are books which must themselves be read by every person who makes any effort to keep up with current literature, and so the briefer notices given in our monthly magazines of the better class, and even those which we find in the great metropolitan dailies, are of very great value as furnishing the information we need about the books which we have no time to read, but concerning which every intelligent man needs to know something.

DANGEROUS READING.

Almost any kind of reading matter, if read to the exclusion of everything else, becomes dangerous. It is never well to cultivate a one-sided mental habit. An intellectual diet, consisting only of poetry, even though the poetry be always of the best, is quite as bad as a physical feeding on nothing but pastry. Dyspepsia, in physical form, is not worse than its intellectual counterpart.

This particular danger is all the greater for the reason that people whose tastes lead them to confine their reading largely to a single kind of literature, are always people whose minds need balancing in precisely the opposite direction. A taste so strong for poetry, or other ideal literature, that its possessor cares for nothing else, indicates a pressing necessity for the cultivation of the more practical faculties. And so it is with every other such leaning.

The student may very properly entertain preferences of this kind, and he is safe enough in allowing them to lead him to a reasonable extent, but he should at all events take pains to preserve the balance which he has cultivated, and whenever he finds his taste leading him into excess in one direction, it is his business at once to restrain and correct it by studies of an opposite character.

I have already advised the cultivation and development of strong points in every case, but strong points become points of weakness if they are allowed to control the whole man.

A little novel-reading may be absolutely necessary to the intellectual equilibrium of a metaphysical or mathematical enthusiast, while there are men and women in whom the reading of fiction has destroyed all that there ever was in them of intellectual vigor, simply because their tendencies and tastes were all in one direction, and no care was taken to turn them in any other.

I cannot too strongly impress upon the student the

necessity of guarding himself against all such dangers. He should know himself as thoroughly as possible, that he may know and supply his own intellectual wants ; but above all, he should see to it that his reading is varied in its character, and that his changes of intellectual food are not left to caprice or chance. He should read some novels, certainly ; a good deal of poetry, without doubt ; some speculative literature ; a good deal of biography, and more of history. If any one class of books please him above the rest, he will certainly read enough of that, but he should take good care that its precise opposite receives a full share of attention.

There is one other danger which comes to every reader. We must all read the newspapers, of course; but to read even one large paper entirely through every day requires a considerable expenditure of time. Now the truth is, that unless one reads newspapers in the way of business, there is very little in one that any one person needs to read. There may be nothing in the paper that should be omitted from it—nothing which will not meet the wants of some reader ; but at the same time the parts that any single individual needs more than he needs the time it would take to read them, are very few and very small. Every reader should learn to find these readily, and he should read nothing else in the paper.

The head-lines and the typographical peculiarities of the several parts will enable an attentive reader to see at a glance what he wants and can afford to read ; but curiosity or carelessness leads nearly all of us to read vastly more of our newspapers than this, to the great wasting of very valuable time. A little care will enable the student to avoid this, and avoid it he must, if he would economize his time properly.

In the reading of magazines and literary papers there is a similar danger, though it exists in much smaller degree, inasmuch as these are more strictly literary in their character, and have therefore no occasion to supply matter of no use to the majority of readers.

A SCHEDULE OF READING-MATTER.

I have already said that set courses of reading are usually valueless, and that it is no part of my purpose to supply anything of the kind. But in carrying out the plan I have suggested, of properly apportioning the different kinds of reading, it will be convenient for the student to keep in mind some distinct classification of literature, more or less elaborate, according to circumstances.

In a general way, the following will answer very well as a basis for such a classification as will be found necessary :

History,	Physical Science,
Biography,	Poetry,
Philosophy,	Fiction,
Travels and Explorations,	Specialties : (*Theology,*
	Law, anything professional.)

The comparative value and importance of these several classes of literature is an indeterminate one, and it varies with the wants, the temperament, the capabilities, and the circumstances of each student.

In a general way, where there are no circumstances making one of these more important than the others, and where the object is simply the improvement of the reader, some attention should be given to each, and the bent of the reader will ordinarily indicate which should enter most largely into the course.

For most readers History (including philosophical essays on historical subjects) should form the larger part of the course, inasmuch as it supplies at once a vast stock of information, and an equally large share of culture .

NOVEL READING.

In point of fact, there will ordinarily be more fiction read than anything else. In our day we have stories and stories, and without entering into any discussion whatever of the merits of novel-reading, I may safely say that most people read too much fiction, and certainly a large part of the fictitious literature of the day—even after excluding all of the trash—is without any especial value to the reader, while the time its perusal occupies greatly limits the amount of other reading possible.

My advice to the student is, to read about half of Dickens's novels ; one or two of George Eliot's ; one or two of Bulwer's best ; most of Scott's—these being history as much as anything else;—Vanity Fair, and one or two others of Thackeray's ; a few of the older English novels of standard reputation, with one or two of the best of our American books of the sort.

There are many others absorbingly interesting and without positively objectionable characteristics of any kind, but life is too short for the reading even of all the *good* novels in print—particularly if the reader wishes to do anything else in the world.

Such a list as the one given above, will occupy as large a portion of time as most of us can afford to give to novel-reading, and the man who has read all, or nearly all, the books mentioned, is as well read in the matter of novels as anybody needs to be, unless his reading is very extensive, in which case a larger amount of fiction would be well enough. A healthful proportion is what we should aim to maintain.

But these should not be read at the beginning of the course, nor should any considerable number of them be read consecutively. It is best first to form a taste for something less exciting, and to avoid impairing that taste afterwards, by an injudicious amount of novel-reading at any one time.

THE READING OF HISTORY.

I have before me, as I write, a letter from a young man who says that his education thus far has been mainly self-conducted, and that having completed his text-book study, he wishes now to become a well-read man. To this end he understands that he must know something of history, and he writes to ascertain how much of history is necessary, "for," continues the letter, "I want to read just as little of dry chronicles as I can get on with."

Now the case of this young man is not an exceptional one by any means. He will never be even a tolerably well-informed person, as a matter of course, unless his ideas shall undergo a radical change, which is hardly probable. But there are two or three mistakes which he makes in common with many other people, and his case furnishes me an opportunity to correct them in the minds of more hopeful students.

In the first place it is no less a mistake to suppose that intelligence may be gotten by an indolent, shirking system of reading, than to imagine that text-books will yield their treasures to the careless and listless student. The man who begins a course of reading with the wish to make it as meagre as possible, is not likely ever to make it of any great value to himself. It is only those who hunger after information that manage to digest it, and the desire and the purpose must be stronger than they seem to be in the mind of my correspondent, before there can be reasonable hope that they will bring about anything like satisfactory results.

There are cases in which the student feels, at first, but little pleasure in reading, but resolutely pursues his course from a strong desire to profit by his labor, and to such the pleasure soon comes to strengthen the purpose.   But when the purpose itself is weak, and no pleasure is felt in the self-imposed task, a vague wish to be well informed, or to appear so, is not sufficient to keep the man at his work, and he might almost as well abandon the purpose in the outset.

A second error is the assumption that history is a matter of dry chronicling.   It is a series of chronicles, of course, but so is every novel, for that matter.   The events in the one case are real, and in the other imaginary, and this far history has the advantage.   There is less of unity in history than in fiction, but as a whole, the former is no less startlingly dramatic than the latter, and to a healthful taste there is quite as much of absorbing interest in true stories of men's deeds as in fictitious ones.

While we are upon the subject of historical reading, let me add a few suggestions which may be of service.

Compends of history are almost worthless as original reading.   To bring them within the required limits it becomes necessary to eliminate nearly everything of value from the narration, and that which is left is but the merest skeleton of the tale they are intended to tell. It is not possible to learn history from books of this sort, and as histories they are worthless. They are to history just what epitomes of English literature are to English literature in its fullness, and properly used they have their value, just as these have theirs in their proper spheres.

It is a very good plan, after the student has completed an extended course of history, either general or special, to take up an abridgment or brief compend, covering the same ground. By this means the course which has been read will be easily reviewed, and the student will have at a single glance a comprehensive view of the whole course over which he has travelled. This is the use, and almost the only good use to which brief historical compends can be put.

I have already pointed out the necessity of reading both sides in history, as in everything else. I must also caution the student against a habit of accepting authority on historical matters unquestioningly.

Passion, prejudice, circumstances of all kinds, enter largely into the telling of the world's story, and he who would get at the truth must weigh carefully the probabilities in every doubtful case, and make due allowance for all these in making up his opinions.

But aside from the fact that such a practice is necessary to the discovery of truth, it is even more important as a habit of mind tending to healthful culture. It exercises the judgment and it cultivates a wholesome habit of doubting and investigating, the value of which can hardly be over-estimated.

In reading history it is well to remember that speculative essays upon historical subjects are quite as important a part of history as the narrative itself, and it
is an excellent plan to follow every course of history
proper with the best essays to be had upon the events
or the men involved.

These sometimes take the shape of biographies—
sometimes they appear as book reviews, and sometimes
they come to us professing to be just what they are.
But whatever their shape, they are peculiarly valuable.
They furnish at once a brief review of the history read,
and a thoughtful commentary upon it.

POETRY.

In reading poetry, the especial purpose, aside from
amusement, is the cultivation of æsthetic feeling.   To
cultivate this worthily it is necessary that everything be
avoided which will tend to warp the taste or to make
it one-sided.   To a great extent we read poetry
only for the sake of the amusement it affords, and to
that extent our selection is dictated by our tastes, but it
is well enough to let the judgment have some control
even here.   I have known ill results to follow from the
too exclusive reading of the works of a single poet
or a single school of poets, and this is the fault against
which I would especially caution the reader.

We need nothing so much as catholicity, both of
opinion and taste, and this can be secured only by
careful culture.

Especially is this true in matters of literary taste.
We not only need to know what different poets have
written, and their several characteristics, but we need,
quite as imperatively, to so far cultivate a catholicity of

taste that we can appreciate the merits and the beauties of each. Our reading of poetry, whether it be a limited or an extensive one, should in any event embrace as large a variety as possible. There are people who appreciate Byron, and Scott, and Shelley, or Pope, and Dryden, and there are others who love Wordsworth, and Longfellow, and Tennyson. Very much smaller is the class of people who love and appreciate all of these and others, but these few are they who see more of beauty in each than the special lovers of each will ever see there, and who are able to set down every singer at his proper valuation.

With this sole caution, I say to the reader, follow the bent of your own taste in the matter of poetry, just as you would in regard to pictures, or any other creations of art. Let your taste be your chief guide in matters of taste, but take care to cultivate it judiciously, in order that it may be a safe and competent guide.

BIOGRAPHY, ETC.

Biography, Travels, Explorations, and similar matters are, to a great extent, but history in another form. The story of a leading man's life is the story of his times. Travels and explorations usually contribute to history, past or present, more than to anything else, and the accounts given of them by the traveller are histories in themselves.

In a general way, what has been said in regard to the study of history applies equally to the reading of books of this sort, except that it should be remembered that biographies and books of travel are often slices of history cut uncommonly thick. If we read an extended biography of any but the very foremost man of his age, we may be devoting to a small segment of the world's history an amount of time wholly out of proportion to its relative importance. And the same thing is true of other books of this class.

As a rule, therefore, it is best to avoid merely historical biographies as a part of historical reading where their subject was not pre-eminently the foremost man of his age—where his story is not wholly the story of his time in some respect.

There is another trouble with biographies, which should be borne constantly in mind while they are in reading, and that is, that the personal element enters very largely into their composition. Men who write biographies do so, very generally, for the purpose of exalting or depreciating the man who forms the subject of their work, or to do the same thing for some measure with which his life was in some way interwoven. They write the man's life because they greatly admire or particularly detest him or his theories, or because they wish to advance some particular end, or for some other reason equally fatal to fairness. Whether conscious of it or not, the writers of this kind of biographies almost always occupy the position of an advocate rather than that of a judge, and this is not the way in which history should be written.

There are, of course, exceptions to this, but they are the exceptions merely, and not the rule, and what I would urge upon the student is the necessity of taking care to give this personal element its full weight in determining the value of conclusions drawn from books of this class.

On the other hand, however, it must be remembered that biography is, to very many people, the most attractive form in which history can be put, and hence its usefulness, as mere history, is very great.

Again, there are biographies not historical—stories of the lives of men whose lives form no part of public history. These are close studies of human development, and form an admirable department of reading by them-selves. To these, what I have said of merely histori-cal biography does not apply at all, and to some extent all written lives of individual men partake of this ex-cellent quality, when the work is at all well done, and from this point of view biography has a value wholly apart from its worth as history.

DICTIONARIES AS READING-MATTER.

The book must be a very bad, or an extremely poor one, which has nothing in it worth reading, when there is nothing better at hand.

There are so many books which we need to read and cannot for want of time, that very many good ones must be left unread, so that we may have time for the ones most imperatively necessary to us. Compara-tively there are vast numbers of books not worth the reading,—positively there are very few, except the trashy ones known as sensational novels.

That is to say, there are very few books which are not well worth the reading when there are no bet-ter ones at hand, and so there will come times to every one of us when we can take up and read books which we should never select where there is room for selection, but which are in themselves worth the reading. It is a good rule never to be caught anywhere without a good supply of reading-matter, but very few of us live strictly up to it. The next best thing is to know how

to make the most of such literature as we can get when
our choice is a very limited one under stress of circumstance.

I remember a strongly illustrative case in point.
I spent nearly a week once in a little village in Ten-
nessee, during a rainy season, when walking out of doors
was simply out of the question. The only books to be
had at all were the Children of the Abbey, Tupper's Proverbial Philosophy, and about one half of an old Johnson's Dictionary.

Doubtless I might have got something out of Tupper,
and possibly a vague shadow of amusement out of the
Children of the Abbey, but the old Dictionary was
by odds the most promising of the three, and I read
it for five consecutive days, making some curious word-
studies in which I became greatly interested. From
that day to this, I have never been at a loss for something to read in any house containing a dictionary, and
I strongly commend all dictionaries and books of that
kind as reading matter of a very interesting and
instructive character. Their value as books of reference
is not their only value by any means, even if this be
their chief use. It will *pay* to go through an unabridged
Webster or Worcester once or twice at least during a
lifetime, not reading everything in it by any means,
but picking out here and there the things one wants.

Still more interesting is a biographical dictionary, or
the dictionary of some technical specialty, if the specialty be one in which the reader feels an interest, and
a good encyclopedia is always a treasure. Not that
anybody should think of reading any one of these
regularly through, or taking it up as set task-work.
But there are odd times when we have nothing else at

hand, or when we care for nothing else for the moment, and at such times one cannot do better than to turn the leaves of a good dictionary, or encyclopedia, in search of something which will strike the fancy.

CHAPTER IX.

A GOOD many of the suggestions I shall give in this concluding chapter follow as corollaries from the teachings already given. Some of them are but recapitulations of the suggestions scattered through former chapters ; others have found no place there.

They are grouped together here for the sake of the student's convenience, and because they constitute a fitting conclusion to my little book.

A PRACTICAL EDUCATION.

The end to be aimed at in every case should, of course, be the securing of as wide and perfect and complete a culture as possible, and the acquisition of as much information as the limits of time and opportunity will allow.

We have already seen that the perfect, ideal education is that which completely and perfectly develops the man, bringing all his faculties into full play, and supplying each with all the information necessary to its very best work.

Practically the best education to be secured is one which falls far short of this, and the best educated people we have are those who know some one thing thoroughly, and have a general acquaintance with others. Practically, this should be the object aimed at by every student, and it should constitute the basis of all his work. But in projecting and pursuing a course of study and reading with this end in view, there is always the danger of giving to the one thing too great a share of attention, and so failing to accomplish the equally important purpose of making one's self acquainted generally with other branches of human knowledge. This danger comes to every student, and it cannot be too carefully avoided.

ECONOMY OF TIME.

Every student whose purpose is in any way a worthy one, will find his time far less abundant than he could wish, and therefore it becomes especially necessary that he shall economize it carefully ; and there are many ways in which this may be done.

Whenever a book is taken up, whether for study as a text-book or only for reading, the purpose it is to serve and the limits of its capacity to serve that purpose, should be distinctly recognized. The student should ask himself—"Why do I want this book ? What can it give me ? How much of it is worth more to me than the time I must give to its reading ?" He should always remember that no book yields anything gratis ; that he pays, in the coin of precious time, for everything he gets out of books, and that it is the worst kind of extravagance to read any book, or any part of any book, which does not yield to the reader something of more value to him than is the time given to the reading. We cannot afford to read even good books when there are better or more necessary ones awaiting our attention. And this is equally true of parts of books. By a little attention to this the student will save a great deal of time. When he shall have read as much of a book as he can afford to read, let him drop it at once, in order that he may have time for others.

A great deal of time is wasted, too, by a habit of inattention, and the student should take the utmost care to avoid the formation of such a habit, or to cure it if it is already formed. It is easy enough to do this, if only the purpose be strong enough. You have only to begin with very short terms of study, letting them be as frequent in their recurrence as possible. Whenever your attention shall flag, make an effort to keep it fixed, and the moment you shall find yourself unable to control it longer, cease to study. Take a walk, work in your garden, or do something else which will rest your mind, and after a brief period of physical exertion, return to your studies. With every return you will be able to fix your attention for a longer period than before, and your habit will soon be cured.

It is always bad to go on reading when the mind is occupied with something else. Such a practice fixes upon the mind and the eye a habit of separate action, which soon becomes chronic, and the habit is fatal to profitable reading.

WHAT TO DO WITH THE MEMORY.

There is a good deal of nonsense talked, concerning the cultivation of the memory, and a good deal of harm done in attempts to develop it abnormally, as well as in making a misuse of it in the study of matters with the real learning of which it has very little to do.

Paradoxical as it may seem, prodigious memories are by no means very rare. "Lightning calculators" have been known almost as long as arithmetic, although they have rarely been men who really knew arithmetic, marvellous as their power of conjuring with figures has always appeared to be to the gaping crowd. The world has always had people whose memories were next to marvellous in their extent and power, and we always shall have them so long as the fact shall remain that almost any person may, if he will, make his memory receive and retain everything, or nearly everything, given to it.

There is nothing easier than the development of a prodigious memory, and there is no faculty of the mind so little worthy of such extreme cultivation.

I once knew a lecturer who vaunted his memory and its performances, as the most marvellous thing with which he was acquainted. He told his audiences how he could not only repeat the Bible from beginning to end, but also give the chapter and verse of any portion if repeated in his presence. He could repeat, also, every conceivable detail of minute geographical fact, and do half a hundred other utterly useless things.

The man was a fool ; but any person of good ordinary capacity can learn all that he learned, by giving as he did a lifetime to the task. The trouble is that the price is worth so much more than the commodity.

But while all this is true, it is also true that a good, trustworthy memory is of very great service, and such a memory is well worth cultivating, within reasonable limits.

HOW TO CULTIVATE THE MEMORY.

If we wish to develop the muscles of any particular part of our bodies, we proceed to exercise those muscles moderately and regularly. It is only by exercise that we can hope to strengthen and improve them.

With the faculties of the mind we do precisely the same thing. If we wish to reason closely and accurately, we must constantly exercise the reasoning faculties. If we wish to develop the mathematical powers of our minds, we must make daily use of mathematical exercises. Now, in this respect, the memory does not differ from the other intellectual faculties, except that its proper cultivation is rather easier than that of most others.

To secure a good memory, therefore, it is only necessary that the student shall exercise it systematically, and we are all doing this every day in a greater or less degree.

We must, however, avoid things which tend to impair the faculty, of which there are several worthy of mention.

THINGS THAT IMPAIR THE MEMORY

Inattention is the first and greatest cause of bad memories, and there was a deal of force in Lord Byron's remark, that he had forgotten his Latin and Greek, "if a man may be said to have forgotten that which he never remembered."

The way in which this habit of inattention is most commonly cultivated is in the careless reading of matters of no importance,—newspaper paragraphs, items,

detached thoughts,—anything which makes no impres-
sion on the reader. The reading of such things gene-
rates a habit of careless, inattentive reading which is
often fatal to anything like a good memory.

The same is true of many other things, which will
readily suggest themselves to the reader, whose rule it
should be, if his memory be defective, never to do anything carelessly or inattentively — even though the
thing done be in itself unworthy of a better doing.

Many people find that while they remember some
things perfectly, they are apt to forget just the ones they
most want to remember. This arises in a large degree
from the total absence of system which is so common in
matters of memory. Even people who carefully classify
and arrange their learning for all other purposes often
omit wholly to do this for the memory, reading and
studying laboriously, but leaving it altogether to chance
what things acquired from the reading and the study
shall be remembered, and what forgotten. That this
is the common practice I think there can be no doubt,
but it is certainly a singularly bad one.

We all know that we can remember any given
thing by "fixing it in the memory" as the phrase has
it,—that is to say, we are all conscious that the memory
may be greatly aided by the formation of a *deliberate
purpose* to remember. Now it is clearly impossible that
we shall make such a deliberate effort for the retention
of every fact and every principle we meet in our study,
reading and observation, and the obvious conclusion is
that we should make some classification of these facts
and principles, so that we may select those which are
most important and make an especial effort to retain

them. A good classification for this purpose is the following :

To be remembered.

To be held ready for reference when wanted.

Not wante further.

Under the first head should come all those things which it is not worth while to remember in detail ; under the second, all those which we need only to remember generally, while we remember just where they may be found when wanted in detail ; under the third, of course, should come everything not worth a special effort of the memory, though many of them will be useful, if remembered without such special effort.

A very fruitful source of failure in attempts to cultivate the memory is the common mistake of confounding the husk with the grain, and learning to retain words rather than the ideas they express. There are many people who readily commit the words of a book to memory whenever they choose, but who after reading a volume find it very difficult to remember anything of its contents, except the passages which have been memorized absolutely. Such memories are provokingly worthless, and yet there are teachers in plenty who take pains to cultivate just such in their pupils.

As a rule, the exact phraseology of a book is never worth remembering, either in whole or in considerable part, and ordinarily it is a waste of time to commit words to memory ; but the mental habit of the student is a very defective one if he fails to retain, in a general way, the ideas of every book read.

In this, as in every other case, it is the thoughts and not the mere words—the kernels and not the shells— that are wanted, and in cultivating the memory, the student needs to look sharply to his processes, lest he cultivate it in the wrong direction. Let him remember that while every faculty is developed by exercise, each is developed strongly in the particular direction in which the exercise points, and that it is therefore espe- cially requisite that he shall make the exercise of his memory a healthful one in kind as well as in amount.

MEMORANDUM BOOKS, ETC.

Memorandum books and other mechanical contri- vances are often useful and sometimes very necessary, but they are susceptible of abuse and capable of work- ing great injury to the memory they are meant to serve. When anything is to be remembered it is so convenient to jot down a note of it, that the plan is of- ten resorted to where the memory itself should be trusted, and the habit of relying upon memoranda ra- ther than upon the memory itself, is often fatal to the proper development of that faculty.

In giving a special caution thus against the abuse of memorandum books, I do so only because these are the commonest forms of artificial aids to memory, but what I say of these is equally true of every other device of the kind, and there are many of them in use. The rule should be the same in all cases, and it should be to use mechanical aids as little as possible, and to carefully observe their effects upon the memory, in order that they may not be allowed to sap it unawares.

I have found it a good plan in my own case, to make memoranda *aids* to memory, rather than substitutes for it. Let me explain what I mean a little more fully. When I particularly wish to remember any isolated fact or other thing, I have no difficulty in doing so, by simply determining that I will. But when I have to collect and remember a considerable number of things for future classification and use, (as, for instance, when collecting and arranging in my mind the materials for an essay or a book,) the unaided memory is not sufficient, and so a resort to memorandum books must be had. In these I jot down brief notes of the things I wish to use, making a rude classification of them as they occur to me from day to day. When this is done I lay the note-books away, and have no occasion whatever to refer to the memoranda in using the material collected. The act of making a written note of any-thing serves to fix the thing in my memory, and ordinarily I have no further use for the note after it is once made.

Now, I do not put this forward as a plan for others' following. Perhaps to most of my readers my contrivances of this sort would be worthless, while others which would work well with them would be of no service to me. In all such matters every man is and must be a law unto himself, and in giving my own plan to the reader I offer it only as a suggestion which may possibly point the way to some device of his own which will similarly serve his purpose.

And just here a general caution is necessary against all attempts to adopt other people's plans in matters of this and like sorts. Nearly all young people try to follow some other person's lead in such matters, and in doing so they almost always fail because the processes of different minds are different.

The only safe course is to let the working rules of other people serve as suggestions for processes adapted to your own wants and your own peculiarities.

And whatever your processes of intellectual work may be, above everything else avoid making your rules or those of other people your masters. They are of service only while they serve, and the moment they assume control over the man, they become tyrants of a particularly objectionable sort.

MECHANICAL MEMORY.

The student will almost certainly meet, sooner or later, with systems of mechanical memory,—elaborate contrivances by which to remember mechanically whatever one wishes to remember without any cultivation of the faculty involved. These systems often contain a few good suggestions for use in the comparatively limited number of cases in which it is possible and desirable to remember things mechanically ; but as systems they are worthless, always, of necessity, and to make any attempt to master one of them is to simply throw away time. They are worthless, in the first place, because of their very elaborateness, which makes it a more difficult task to master them than it would be to cultivate the memory itself to a far greater degree of precision than the systems can justly claim. In the second place, with all their seeming completeness, they usually fail just where they are needed most. Thirdly, it is generally more difficult to remember their devices for remembering things than it would be to remember the things themselves. But, after all, the chief difficulty with all these systems lies in the fact that they aim only at the recollection of words,-- they deal only with the husks of knowledge, and hence are inherently unworthy.

HOW MUCH TO READ.

Students are often led to inquire how much they should read within a month or a year, and answers of all sorts have been given to the question.

In this as in other matters of a similar nature it is impossible to give an estimate worth anything, or one which will be even approximately correct in a majority of cases.

The general principle is, that we should not read more than we can digest ; but what would be a surfeit for one intellect is wholly insufficient for the ordinary food of another. Moreover, it is difficult for the reader to discover just how perfectly or imperfectly he has assimilated his intellectual food.

Again, we may store the mind to-day with information to be digested long hence, and the fact that we have not yet made positive use of all that we have read is not proof that we have read too much.

In point of fact, very few people read too much. Most of us read far too little, and the student need have very little apprehension on the score of an intellectual surfeit. The appetite is in this case a pretty safe guide, and in a very large majority of cases it may be freely indulged, as to amount, without any kind of danger, if only the reading be of a proper sort.

WHEN TO READ.

" Is it best to have fixed times at which to read?" asks a young man in a letter now lying before me.

I answer Yes, and No.

It is certainly best to have fixed times for reading if,

without them, the reading is likely to be neglected to any considerable extent. It is best to have rules for your own guidance and control *if you need them.* Other-wise, certainly not.

It is no small part of education to learn to govern one's self, but that self-government which accomplishes its purpose with the smallest amount of law is best. Government is necessary in every case, but the freer it can have its subject the better it will be for him.

In all matters of this sort, therefore, the student should proceed as best he can, taking care first that his duties to himself in the matter of study and reading are fully and fairly performed, and secondly, that he remains as largely a free agent as is consistent with the accomplishment of this end. He should make rules for himself, and enforce them strictly too, if rules are necessary to him, but if he can perform all his duties to himself without limitations of this kind, it will be far better not to hedge himself about with self-imposed and unnecessary statutes.

THE PROPER TIME OF DAY FOR READING AND STUDY.

As to what is the proper time of day for intellectual work of any kind, opinions differ largely among people who have strong prejudices or preferences in the matter —each thinking that his own favorite time is in every way the best.

Probably habit has as much to do with it as anything else, in most cases ; and surrounding circumstances ordinarily determine the question for all of us.

Except that the health should be carefully guarded, the best possible rule, doubtless, is to do your reading

and studying when you can do it best—in the morning
—at night—or at whatever other time you find to be
the best in your own case.

It is important, however, to learn to read, to study
and to write quite as well in the midst of interruptions
as anywhere else. This anybody may learn to do with
a little practice, and it is well worth the learning, even
to people who have abundant and uninterrupted leisure.

THOUGHT STUDY.

During all our waking hours we are thinking of
something. The moment we cease to think, we are
asleep.

This fact is well enough known to everybody, but its
lesson is not always learned. We go on thinking,
thinking, thinking, but how many of us make a systematic effort to so control our thoughts as to make them of
value to us?

When we walk in the streets, or ride in the cars, or
do anything else which leaves our minds free, we are
very apt to let them run on listlessly from one subject
to another without care, and the result is that all our
thinking—all this wearing labor of our brains produces
nothing of any value to us, except it be by accident.

But this loss of intellectual labor is not the only ill
result of allowing the thoughts to run riot among tri-
vialities. We need to form habits of self-control. Such
habits constitute at least half of culture, and their ex-
istence is absolutely necessary to the accomplishment of
anything like satisfactory educational results. We
must control our intellectual operations, if we would
train our intellects to satisfactory and systematic activ-

ity, and there is nothing so fatal to such control as is this habit of loose, unguided, random thinking.

The mind must have rest, of course, but the rest comes from change and from sleep—not from uncontrolled and useless activity. For these reasons I strongly urge upon the student the habit of thought-study, as it is sometimes called. Let him always have some subject or other ready for consideration, and when nothing else offers, let him think about that, taking care that his thinking shall be systematic. Let him also cultivate the habit of self-control to such an extent that he may dismiss one subject and take up another at will. Then let him question everything about him for information and for culture. He will soon find that he can learn quite as much from men and things as from books.

As a rule, it is better that we should observe the men and the things about us, and think of them, than that we abstract ourselves, and hence it is best to keep the chosen subject in reserve so long as there are other things at hand to furnish food for thought. This habit of observing our surroundings and thinking about them furnishes us the very best possible object-lessons, and it is this very habit which has resulted in some of the greatest of human achievements. A very simple thing indeed, to furnish food for thought, is a tea-kettle lid, but because James Watt, when he saw it, thought about it, we have now our steam-engine, and this one man's habit of object-study advanced the civilization of the world incalculably. History is full of just such illustrations, and if we could always trace these things accurately, we should almost certainly find that every man who accomplishes anything of moment to himself or to the world, owes his success to habits of this character.

There are other mental habits, some to be cultivated and some to be shunned, and these for the most part will suggest themselves and sufficiently indicate their natures to the student who takes himself in hand for training. One or two of them, however, may be mentioned

It is a good plan to doubt and investigate. Doubt is the forerunner of wisdom, and there is no worse habit of mind than that which prompts the easy acceptance of professed facts without proof. Authority is only good in so far as it is authority, and it should be accepted no farther. When I read in my chemistry that oxygen, hydrogen and carbon are elementary subtances, the authority of the eminent chemist who tells me this is sufficient to convince me that this is a correct statement of the fact so far as the fact is understood by the chemists, but in holding myself ready to believe that all these substances may after all be compounds, and may ultimately be discovered to be such, I only do precisely what the chemists themselves do, and what they must of necessity do if they hope to make any new discoveries in their science. An unreasoning and dogmatic skepticism is as bad as an unreasoning credulity, but the habit of holding the mind open to conviction, and the habit of questioning everything for the sake of learning more about it are certainly exceedingly valuable ones.

Just here it is necessary to caution the reader against a bad habit into which a good many people fall, and that is the habit of accepting the statement of a puzzling fact and trying to account for it before ascertaining that the fact is as it is stated, or in any other way beginning at the wrong end of an investigation.

There is an old story of a puzzling question as to why a living fish put into a vessel of water does not add to the weight of the whole. A good deal of speculation was had on the subject and many ingenious theories advanced by way of explanation. I believe it was Dr. Franklin who solved it, by first putting a living fish into a vessel of water to learn whether or not the assumption on which the question was based was a true one.

The Patent Office at Washington is full of failures which have consumed men's lives in the making, and in nine cases out of ten they are failures only because their inventors omitted to examine and verify the terms of the problems they tried to solve.

Every sleight of hand juggler depends upon this habit of men's minds for success in his deceptions. He sets people to puzzling over seeming facts which are not facts at all, and they, having begun at the wrong end of their investigations, might continue them till doomsday without coming a step nearer to the truth of which they are in search.

I have sometimes amused myself testing the question of how nearly universal this habit is. There is an absurdly simple trick with cards, which ought to deceive nobody, and yet it will deceive about eight people out of every ten, even when bunglingly performed. It is to arrange a pack of cards with the three spot of any suite at the bottom, and then to give the person with whom you are experimenting the ace of that suite, bidding him slip it into the pack as it lies, face downwards, on the

table.   When he shall have done this, take up the pack,
hold its face toward you, place your two thumbs over
two of the three spots on the card next to you, blow, or
say something, and exhibit the ace at the bottom of the
pack.   Every intelligent man must know that this card
which he sees cannot possibly be the ace which he has
just slipped into another place, and yet I have seen this
simple trick performed over and over again in the presence of intelligent men and women, every one of whom
would set about finding out *how* it was done, not one of
them ever thinking to inquire whether or not it really
was done.

Now, this is precisely what we all do every day to a
greater or less extent, and as the habit greatly interferes
with successful investigation in daily life, I have thought
it worthy of notice in this place.

THE APPORTIONMENT OF TIME.

A great deal of advice has been wasted on the subject
of apportionment of time between study, work, sleep,
etc.   We all remember Dr. Franklin's dictum on the
subject, and we all see various modifications of it in the
newspapers now and then.

Now if there were no other reason for saying that
none of these prearranged schedules are worth anything,
we should find amply sufficient justification for such a
remark in the fact that hardly any two people agree as
to the proportions to be maintained.   Dr. Franklin
thought six hours sleep per day enough for a man ; but
Mr. Beecher, who does quite as much work, probably,
as Dr. Franklin did, sleeps, we are told, twelve hours
out of twenty-four ordinarily, and never denies himself
an additional " forty winks" when he wants them.

The fact seems to be that in this, as in everything else, men differ materially from each other. Some require more sleep than others, just as some require more food. Some can stand many hours of continuous labor, while others must have frequent spells of resting.

The only good rule in such a case is for each student to be a law unto himself. There is no extravagance so disastrous as the economy which denies to the student any needed sleep, whether the term allotted to perfect rest be four hours or twelve. Get all the sleep you need,—eat as much as you want,—and never continue your studies so long at a sitting as to leave yourself with a prostrated, worn-out feeling, as the result.

Of course I do not advise unlimited self-indulgence. We must be masters of ourselves, both in body and mind, if we would accomplish anything in life. Reason must be our guide, and reason should always hold supremacy over impulse. But if we wish to get the fullest measure of work out of an animal, we take care that he has rest enough and food enough to repair all waste. If we have machinery at work for us, we care for it similarly, in order that it may not wear out and cease to be of service. Now this is precisely what we must do with our bodies and minds. We must repair their waste places,—we must keep them in working order, and give them rest enough and food enough to keep up their strength, else they will inevitably break down, more or less entirely.

But in the matter of rest, a good deal of time may be saved by a little care. Change is in itself rest, and it often serves the purpose better than an attempted cessation from work would. When one is greatly interested in the work in hand, it is very often impossible to dismiss it at once from the mind, and to simply quit the reading of a book is not always to rest from the reading. The subject is still in the mind, and the mind works at it quite as actively without the book as with it. It is always best, where this is the case, if rest is needed, to take up some book of a wholly different character for a while before ceasing to read entirely, so that the mind may be drawn away from the matter with which it is wearied.

There are many times, too, when it is not necessary to quit work at all—times when a simple change of work gives all the relief the mind needs, and a little attention to this fact will make it a great economizer of time.

HOW MANY STUDIES SHOULD BE CARRIED ON AT ONCE?

There is considerable difference of opinion as to the number of studies that should be pursued at once. In the colleges the number usually prescribed is from three to five, and I am certainly not prepared to say that five are too many or three too few ; but I have known students to accomplish most excellent results by taking a single branch and pushing it through to the end of the course before taking up another. I have known others to carry on as many as nine separate studies at once, doing thoroughly well in all. The result in the end was as good in the one case as in the other.

Probably the safest plan is to accept the college custom as the proper rule in the matter, and to regard these cases as successful exceptions. Certainly, there are objections to either extreme, and the more moderate three, four or five studies furnish enough of variety to enable the student to rest by changing from one to the other, while they do not weaken his attention by dividing it too much.

After all, the student cannot do better than attend to the teachings of the colleges in details of this charac-ter, and where their practice is at all uniform it will generally be found to represent the best plan of pro-cedure even for the student without a master.

THE END